Olive Green:
Learning English through a Mystery Drama
(CEFR-A1)

CEFR A1

ASARI Yoko

KANNO Satoru

KUBO Takeo

SATO Ryosuke

Asahi Press

音声再生アプリ「リスニング・トレーナー」を使った音声ダウンロード

朝日出版社開発のアプリ、「リスニング・トレーナー（リストレ）」を使えば、教科書の音声をスマホ、タブレットに簡単にダウンロードできます。どうぞご活用ください。

◉ アプリ【リスニング・トレーナー】の使い方

《アプリのダウンロード》

App Store または Google Play から「リスニング・トレーナー」のアプリ（無料）をダウンロード

App Storeはこちら▶

Google Playはこちら▶

《アプリの使い方》

① アプリを開き「コンテンツを追加」をタップ
② 画面上部に【15674】を入力しDoneをタップ

音声・映像ストリーミング配信 》》》

この教科書の音声及び、付属の映像は、右記ウェブサイトにて無料で配信しています。

https://text.asahipress.com/free/english/

はじめに

　本書は、映画Olive Greenを題材とし、学習者のリスニング能力とスピーキング能力の
さらなる向上を目的として作成されました。

　この映画は英語学習用に特別に撮り下ろされ、CEFRに準拠しつつ文法事項が導入され
ています。この映画を繰り返し見ることにより、学習者は過度な負担を感じることなく、
リスニング能力のレベルアップを行うことが可能となります。また、各シーンの会話部分
のみを録音し直している音源もあり、明瞭な音声で聞きたい場合やディクテーションの際
に活用することができます。

　各Chapterにはスピーキング練習用のアクティビティも豊富に含まれています。スピー
キング・アクティビティは、そのChapterで導入された文法項目の学習を意図しています。
ペア・ワーク、グループ・ワークを通し、学習者はスピーキング能力を向上させることが
できます。

　リスニングとスピーキングの2つの能力は、日本人学習者にとって苦手とされてきまし
たが、実際の言語使用においては必要不可欠です。また、近年では、多くの英語検定試験
でこの2つの能力を測るテストが導入されています。本書を通し、技能向上の一助となる
ことを願っております。

執筆者一同

■各Chapterの構成 ✿

本書のChapterは主に次のものから成り立っています。

The target of this chapter is to understand:

学習する文法事項が最初に示されています。どのような文法事項を学習するのか、初めに確認しておきましょう。

Review Activity

1つ前のChapterで導入された文法事項を復習するためのアクティビティです。主に、ペア・ワークを使ったスピーキング・アクティビティとなっています。

Warm-Up

学習する映画のシーンを見る前に、Warm-Upとして、どの部分に注目すればよいかが導入されています。日本語で2つの質問が書かれていますので、映像を見る前に質問に答えてみましょう。

Let's Watch!

映画のシーンを理解するのに必要となる単語・句・文が掲載されています。あらかじめ発音・意味などを確認しておきましょう。また、この部分には、スクリプトの一部が空欄で提示されています。ディクテーション用のアクティビティとしても活用できます。

Comprehension Check

さまざまな内容確認用の問題を通し、それぞれのシーンの内容を確認することができます。

Grammar

それぞれのChapterで焦点が当てられている文法事項を確認してください。学習する文法事項はCEFRにおおむね準拠しています。

Speaking Activity

スピーキング用のアクティビティが掲載されています。ペア・ワークやグループ・ワークを通し、スピーキングの練習をしていきましょう。

Role Play

Chapterの内容と関連する2人の人物の会話が載っています。発展的な内容となっており、シーンでは含めることができなかった単語・表現を練習する機会となります。

Contents

Olive Green

Learning English
through a Mystery Drama

CEFR-A1

Asahi Press

Chapter 1

Job Offer

The target of this chapter is to understand:

- *Be*-verb in present simple（現在形のbe動詞）
- Subject pronouns（人称代名詞）
- Possessive pronouns（所有格代名詞）
- Indefinite articles (*a* / *an*) with singular or plural nouns（不定冠詞と単数形名詞／複数形名詞）

Warm-Up

まずは音を消して映像だけ見てみましょう。その後、pairを作り、次の点を話し合いましょう。

- 女性の部屋には何がありましたか？
- 彼女はどこの国にいると思いますか？
- どのようなストーリーだと思いますか？
- 彼女の職業は何だと思いますか？

1

2

3

4

Let's Watch!

Scene 1-1

CD: Track **02** / DVD: Chapter **01** (00:00-01:07)

Words and Phrases

full name: My full name is _____.
nationality: Her nationality is Japanese.
American: an American from New York.
age: at the age of six
talented: a talented musician
thief: a car thief
boss: She is a powerful boss.
complicated: a complicated problem
things: Things are different now.

between: a secret between us
price on one's head:
  There is a price on the killer's head.
alone: alone in a room
broke: I am broke, so I can't buy anything.
in one's opinion:
  In my opinion, it's a good book.
perfect: a perfect example
young: a young child

Script of the Scene

Client: Her [1](   ) name is Gabriella Aguilar. A-G-U-I-L-A-R.
Nationality: [2](   ). Age: [3](   ). She is a very talented
[4](   ) thief. Her [5](   ) is Dieter Kirsch, but things are
complicated between them now and [6](   ) a price on her
[7](   ). She [8](   ) alone and broke. In my
[9](   ), she is perfect!

Client: [10](   ) so young ... but okay!

Scene 1-2

CD: Track **03** / DVD: Chapter **02** (01:07-01:41)

Words and Phrases

what's the word:
  My ex-boyfriend is—what's the word—crazy.
consultant: an IT consultant
funny: a funny comedian

well: Well, actually, I'm a thief.
client: a company client
job: a new job
offer: a kind offer

Script of the Scene

Client: Ms Aguilar? Gabriella Aguilar? [11](   ) [12](   )
         [13](   )?

Gabriella: Who [14](   ) you?

Client: Ms Aguilar – an art ... what's the word?

Gabriella: Consultant. I'm [15](   ) [16](   ) consultant.

Client: Consultant? Yes, that's [17](   ) funny! Well, I'm
         [18](   ) new client. A [19](   ) client with a great
         [20](   ) offer.

3

Words and Phrases

be interested: I'm interested in music.

be on vacation: He is on vacation in Hawaii.

flat: live in a flat

be in trouble: Are you in trouble?

really: I'm really sorry I'm late.

prison: get out of prison

because of...:
  School was cancelled because of the snow.

murderer: The murderer killed two people.

fault: The mistake was my fault.

be after: The police are after a thief in this town.

dangerous: dangerous animals

these days:
  My parents look happy these days.

way out: a way out to the exit

locker: a locker room

airport: Let's meet at the airport.

passport:
  Bring your passport to the airport.

photo: take a photo

All right: All right! I understand.

enough: Stop it! That's enough!

Script of the Scene

Gabriella: I'm not interested. ²¹(   ) on vacation.

....

Client: Ms Aguilar? You're ²²(   ) on vacation.
           You're in your ²³(   ) in 9 Greenwood Avenue, Brooklyn.
           And ²⁴(   ) in trouble.

Gabriella: ²⁵(   ) I really?

Client: Oh yes! Kirsch, your boss, is in prison ... ²⁶(   )
           ²⁷(   ) you.

Gabriella: He's in prison because ²⁸(   ) a murderer.

Client: Well ... but it is your fault and his men are after you!
           The USA is a very ²⁹(   ) place for you these days.
           But ³⁰(   ) ³¹(   ) a way out!

Gabriella: What way out?

Client: There is a locker at JFK Airport with a passport inside. Your
           ³²(   ) is on it. And ³³(   ) new ³⁴(   ) ...
           Olive Green.

Gabriella: All right! ³⁵(   )! What's the job?

Comprehension Check

Exercise 1 True (T) or false (F)?

1. (   ) Gabriella is rich.

2. (   ) Her boss is on vacation.

3. (   ) The police are after Gabriella.

4. (   ) Kirsch is her client.

5. (   ) She gets a new name.

6. (   ) She accepts the offer.

Exercise 2 Answer the following questions.

1. Is Gabriella in trouble?   (   )

2. What is the name of her boss?   (   )

3. Where is her flat? In the UK or the USA? (   )

4. What is her job?   (   )

5. Is she interested in the offer?   (   )

6. Where is her new passport?   (   )

7. What is her new name?   (   )

Exercise 3 Put the sentences in the correct order.

1. Her client calls.

2. She accepts the offer.

3. She comes back to her flat.

4. She gets the phone call again.

5. She hangs up the phone.

6. She opens the suitcase.

_____ → _____ → _____ → _____ → _____ → _____

Subject pronouns and *be*-verb

	positives	negatives	questions	answers
Singular	I am (I'm) a thief.	I'm not a thief.	Am I an art thief?	Yes, I am. No, I'm not.
	You are (You're) a student.	You aren't a student.	Are you a student?	Yes, you are. No, you aren't.
	He/She is (He's/She's) a teacher.	He/She isn't a teacher.	Is he/she a teacher?	Yes, he/she is. No, he/she isn't.
	It is (It's) a dog.	It isn't a dog.	Is it a dog?	Yes, it is. No, it isn't.
Plural	We are (We're) students.	We aren't students.	Are we students?	Yes, we are. No, we aren't.
	You are (You're) art collectors.	You aren't art collectors.	Are you art collectors?	Yes, you are. No, you aren't.
	They are (They're) consultants.	They aren't consultants.	Are they consultants?	Yes, they are. No, they aren't.

Possessive pronouns

singular			plural		
I	➜ my	It's my phone.	we	➜ our	Our passports are in the locker.
you	➜ your	What's your name?	you	➜ your	Your jobs are interesting.
he	➜ his	His nationality is British.			
she	➜ her	Her boss is Dieter Kirsch.	they	➜ their	Olive is their new art consultant.
it	➜ its	I like its color.			

Articles

a / an I am a student. (1 student)

before the vowel sound: *a, e, i, o, u* e.g., It's an interesting job offer. / I'm an artist.

but: We are ~~a/an~~ students. (2, 3... students)

Exercise 1 Fill in the blanks with the correct form.

1. A: (   ) you Japanese?

    B: Yes, I am. (   ) from Tokyo.

2. A: (   ) you teachers?

    B: No, we (   ). (   ) police officers.

3. A: (   ) it your umbrella?

    B: No, it (   ) not (   ) umbrella. It's John's.

4. A: (   ) they her books?

    B: Yes, they (   ) (   ) books.

Exercise 2 Change the sentences by following the directions.

e.g., *I'm a student.*   *Negative: I'm not a student.*

1. They are his brothers.   Negative: (   )

                                       Question: (   )

2. It is a photo of this town. Negative: (   )

                                       Question: (   )

3. Is she your consultant? Positive: (   )

Exercise 3 Change the underlined word(s) with the word(s) in parentheses.

e.g., *I'm a student. (We)* → *We are students.*

1. <u>You</u> are a university student. (I)

    (   )

2. <u>She</u> is an art thief. (They)

    (   )

3. It is <u>a book</u>. (old book)

    (   )

4. It is your <u>pen</u>. (pens)

    (   )

5. This is <u>my</u> passport. (your)

    (   )

Speaking Activity

Exercise 1

Ask and answer the following questions with your partner(s).

1. Is your teacher from Australia?
2. Are you sometimes late for class?
3. Is your university far from your home?
4. Are you interested in comic books?
5. Are you and your parents alike?
6. Ask your own question with *Is/Are...?*.

Exercise 2

Look at the pictures and try to make as many sentences as possible with your partner(s).

e.g., *A tablet is on the table.*

1.   Picture 1

Useful expressions: tablet, books, notebook, piece of paper, phone

2.   Picture 2

Useful expressions: alone, on the phone, on the wall, flag, armchair

Role Play

CD Track 05

James: Hi, I'm James.

Lisa: Nice to meet you. Where are you from?

James: I come from Europe.

Lisa: Oh, Europeans are always interesting to me. I'm American. And you? Are you German or French?

James: No, I am Polish.

Lisa: And what do you do there?

James: I'm a teacher.

Lisa: So, you work at a school. Can I visit you?

James: Yes, you can. No problem.

Lisa: What's your email address?

James: My email is: E-V-E-@hotmail.com.

Lisa: Thank you. Speak soon.

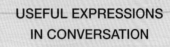

USEFUL EXPRESSIONS IN CONVERSATION

Nice to meet you.

Where are you from?

No problem.

What's your ...?

Thank you.

[Chapter
2]

The Murrays

The target of this chapter is to understand:
- Demonstrative pronouns *(this / that / these / those)* （指示代名詞）
- *Have got* in positive sentences and question sentences （have gotを含む文）
- Possessive *'s*: singular noun＋*'s* / plural noun＋*'* （所有格の'ｓ）

Warm-Up

1. あなたの趣味は何ですか？
2. 好きな画家はいますか？

Warm-Up

DVDを見て、次の質問に英語で答えてみましょう。

1. Who are they?
2. What are their jobs?
3. What are their relationships?
4. How old are they?

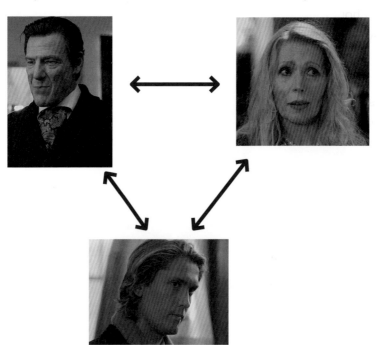

Scene 2-1

CD: Track 06 / DVD: Chapter 04 (03:25-04:27)

Words and Phrases

town: a seaside town

nothing special:
  It's nothing special, but this is for you.

stone circles: visit the stone circles

near: near the river

officially: You are officially husband and wife.

work: hard work

archaeology: study archaeology at university

Script of the Scene

That is the town of Old Berry. A nice, ¹(   ) town. Nothing special, really.
²(   ) ³(   ) the stone circles near the town. Officially, they
are your work... because Olive Green ⁴(   ) now a ⁵(   ) of
archaeology from the USA.

Scene 2-2

CD: Track 07 / DVD:Chapter 05 (04:27-05:04)

Words and Phrases

manor: a manor house

bedroom: My house has two bedrooms.

library: study in the library

businessman: a successful businessman

clever: a clever dog

son: She has three sons.

have got: I've got a nice pen.

important: an important meeting

hobby: My hobby is cooking.

drinking: a drinking habit

woman: Those women are my sisters.

maiden name: Her maiden name is _____.

housewife: a full-time housewife

gardening: do some gardening

Script of the Scene

This is Campbell Manor. It's got 22 bedrooms, a big ⁶(   ) and a park.
⁷(   ) ⁸(   ) Robert Murray. Age: 55. Job: businessman. A
clever and dangerous man. That is Robert Murray's son, Curtis. Age: ⁹(   ).
He ¹⁰(   ) ¹¹(   ) a job, but he's got two important
¹²(   ): drinking and women. ¹³(   ) ¹⁴(   ) Beatrice
Murray, maiden name: Campbell. She is Curtis's ¹⁵(   ) and the wife of
Robert Murray. Age: 46. She's a ¹⁶(   ). Her hobby is gardening.

 **Words and Phrases**

painting: oil paintings

famous: a famous artist

collection: a large collection of books

thistle: The thistle is the Scottish flower.

impressionist: an impressionist painter

masterpiece: This book is a real masterpiece.

worth: It's worth one billion yen.

maybe: He is maybe 35 years old.

million: one million yen

pound:
change Japanese yen to British pounds

steal: steal money from someone

Script of the Scene

These [17]( ) are the famous Murray collection. And this is "Thistle Flowers."

It's an impressionist masterpiece. [18]( ) [19]( ) it's worth 25,

maybe 30, million pounds. Your job is to [20]( ) this painting for me.

Comprehension Check

Exercise 1 True (T) or false (F)?

1. ( ) Old Berry is a big city.

2. ( ) The stone circles are far from Old Berry.

3. ( ) Olive Green's major is archaeology.

4. ( ) Campbell Manor has more than 20 bedrooms.

5. ( ) Robert is a businessman.

6. ( ) Beatrice is Curtis's sister.

Exercise 2 Answer the following questions.

1. Has Campbell Manor got a big library? ( )

2. Who is Curtis? ( )

3. What is Curtis's hobby? ( )

4. Whose hobby is gardening? ( )

5. Has Robert got an impressionist masterpiece?

    ( )

6. Has Olive got "Thistle Flowers"? ( )

Exercise 3 What are these pictures?

1. This is _____.

2. Those are the _____.

3. That is _____.

4. This is _____.

Grammar

Demonstrative pronouns: *this / that / these / those*

Singular	Plural
This: This is Campbell Manor. ☞●	These: These are the paintings. ☞●●●
That: That is Old Berry. ☞　　　　　●	Those: Those are stone circles. ☞　　　　　●●●

Have got / Has got

Singular	Plural
I have got (I've got) an English textbook.	We have got (We've got) an art collection.
You have got (You've got) a Toyota car.	You have got (You've got) a nice house.
He has got (He's got) a famous painting. She has got (She's got) a garden. It has got (It's got) 22 bedrooms.	They have got (They've got) many rooms in their manor.

Question sentences

I/You/We/They **have got** a famous painting.	→ **Have** I/you/we/they **got** a famous painting?
He/She/It **has got** many flowers in the garden.	→ **Has** he/she/it **got** many flowers in the garden?

Answers

Have you **got** an apartment in Old Berry?	→ Yes, I **have**. I've **got** a small apartment. → No, I **haven't**. I've **got** a room in a B&B.
Has Curtis **got** a job?	→ Yes, he **has**. He **has got** two jobs. → No, he **hasn't**. But he's **got** two hobbies.

Possessive *'s*

→ singular noun + **'s**	What is Olive's job? / This is Jessica's house.
→ plural noun + **'**	These are my sons' passports.
→ two nouns + **'s**	Curtis is Beatrice and Robert's son. Campbell Manor is Beatrice and Robert's family home.

Exercise 1 Fill in the blanks with *have got* or *has got*.

1. A: (   ) they got an apartment?

    B: Yes, they (   ). (   ) got a nice apartment.

2. A: (   ) she got a car?

    B: No, she (   ), but she (   ) got a motorbike.

3. A: (   ) you (   ) a pen?

    B: No, but I (   ) got a pencil.

4. A: (   ) you got a laptop?

    B: Yes, I (   ). My wife and I (   ) also got a desktop.

Exercise 2 Change the underlined word(s) with the words in parentheses.

e.g., _This_ is a house. (These) → _These are houses._

1. This is a painting. (These)

   ( )

2. Those are pictures. (That)

   ( )

3. This is a book. (old books)

   ( )

4. These are impressionist masterpieces. (This)

   ( )

Exercise 3 Rewrite the sentences with possessive -'s.

e.g., _This pen belongs to Curtis._ → _This is Curtis's pen._

1 This book belongs to Susan.

   ( )

2. These pens and pencils belong to my brother.

   ( )

3. That masterpiece belongs to Victoria and Charles.

   ( )

4. Those photos belong to my parents.

   ( )

Speaking Activity

Exercise 1

Ask and answer the following questions with your partner(s).

1. Have you got any pets?

2. Have you got a part-time job?

3. Have you got a laptop in your bag?

4. Have your parents got a car?

5. Has your teacher got blond hair?

6. Ask your own question with *have* (*has*) + *got*.

Exercise 2.1

Look at the family tree below. Fill in the blanks. Then check your answers with your partner(s).

e.g., *James is (Susan) and (George's) son.*

1. Taylor is (   ) wife.

2. Olivia is (   ) and (   ) daughter.

3. Susan and Emily are (   ) grandmothers.

4. George is (   ) father-in-law.

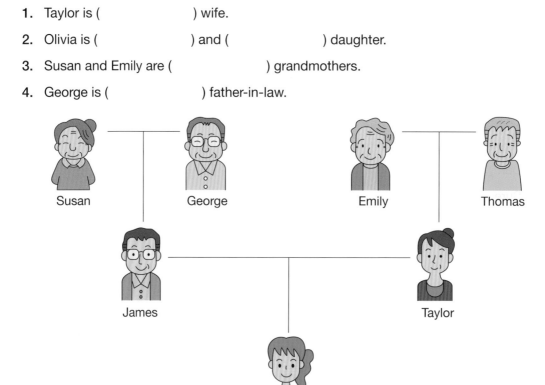

16

Exercise 2.2

Draw your family tree in the space below. Show and explain your family to your partner(s).

Exercise 3

Take three items from your bag and put them on the table. Look at your partner's items. Make sentences with *this / that / these / those.*

e.g., *This is an eraser. Those are notebooks.*

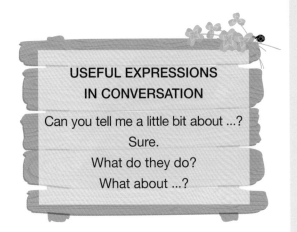 CD: Track 09

Role Play

A: Can you tell me a little bit about your family?

B: Sure.

A: Have you got any brothers or sisters?

B: Yes, I've got a brother and a sister.

A: What do they do?

B: My brother is an IT consultant.

A: And what about your sister?

B: My sister is a police officer.

USEFUL EXPRESSIONS
IN CONVERSATION

Can you tell me a little bit about ...?
Sure.
What do they do?
What about ...?

Old Berry's Best B&B

The target of this chapter is to understand:

・Present simple（一般動詞現在形の肯定文）

・Negatives in present simple（一般動詞現在形の否定文）

・Time expressions in present simple（時の表現）

・Third person singular -*s*（三単現のs）

Review Activity

写真に合う適切な指示代名詞をカッコ内に入れましょう。
(Fill in the blanks with *this / that / these / those*.)

1. (　　　　) is a camera.

2. (　　　　) is a BMW.

3. (　　　　) are pictures.

4. (　　　　) are heavy machines.

Warm-Up

1. B&Bに泊まったことはありますか？

2. B&Bではどのような人が働いていますか？

Let's Watch!

Scene 3-1

CD: Track 10 / DVD: Chapter 07 (05:26-06:20)

 Words and Phrases

Good morning.: Good morning, everyone.

luv (love): Do you want some coffee, luv?

broken: His arm is broken.

book: book a hotel room

right here: Stay right here.

reservation: make a reservation

until: until five o'clock

next: See you next week.

Friday: a Friday night

Silly me!: Silly me! I forgot my wallet.

run: run a restaurant

single: a single man

Excuse me?: Excuse me. Is this your pen?

mind: I don't mind.

want: I want to sleep.

find: I can't find my glasses.

Script of the Scene

Jessica: Good morning, ¹(   ). Sorry, that thing is broken!

Olive: Good morning. My ²(   ) Olive Green. I have a room booked here.

Jessica: Yes, yes, I have your ³(   ) right here. You're here until next

⁴(   ), aren't you? Oh, sorry, ⁵(   ) ⁶(   )

– I'm Jessica.

I ⁷(   ) the place.

....

Olive: Yes?

Jessica: Nothing. Are you ⁸(   )?

Olive: ⁹(   ) ¹⁰(   )?

Jessica: Are you single?

David: Don't mind my mother. She ¹¹(   ) to find a wife for me.

Words and Phrases

hi: Hi, how're you doing?

meet: meet new people

too: Me too.

be a good boy: Be a good boy, my dear.

take: take him to the hospital

luggage: carry luggage

Boy!: Boy! It's so hot!

heavy: a heavy bag

weapon: dangerous weapons

explosive: nuclear explosives

Just kidding!: Just kidding! Forget it.

Script of the Scene

David: Hi, I'm David. ¹²(   ) to ¹³(   ) you.

Olive: I'm Olive. Nice to meet you, ¹⁴(   ).

Jessica: David, be a good boy and take Ms Green's ¹⁵(   ) to her room.

David: Boy, it's ¹⁶(   )! What have you got inside? Weapons and explosives?

David: Just ¹⁷(   ). Okay. Let's go. It's Room 5.

Comprehension Check

Exercise 1 True (T) or false (F)?

1. (   ) Olive has got a reservation.

2. (   ) Jessica asks Olive's age.

3. (   ) David is a successful businessman.

4. (   ) Olive's bag is not heavy.

5. (   ) David carries Olive's bag for her.

Exercise 2 Answer the following questions.

1. Is David single? ( )
2. Where is Olive? ( )
3. What does Jessica do? ( )
4. Has Olive got light luggage? ( )
5. What is Olive's room number? ( )

Exercise 3 Put the sentences in the correct order.

1. David picks up the luggage.
2. David says hello to Olive.
3. Jessica asks a personal question.
4. Jessica introduces herself.
5. Olive arrives at the B&B.
6. Olive enters her room.

_____ → _____ → _____ → _____ → _____ → _____

Grammar

Present simple

→ habits, routine	Olive robs art collections. / You study with this textbook. Tourists visit Old Berry every summer.
→ facts	Water boils at 100°C. / The earth goes around the sun.

Third person singular (*he / she / it*)

• In general, verb + s	e.g., work → works, take → takes, enjoy → enjoys
• s, ss, z, ch, sh, x, o → es	e.g., watch → watches, finish → finishes, do → does
• consonant + y → y̶ + ies	e.g., study → studies, cry → cries

Positives and negatives in present simple

	positives	negatives
singular	I run this place.	I do not (don't) run this place.
	You work in a hospital.	You do not (don't) work in a hospital.
	He/She/It listens to music.	He/She/It does not (doesn't) listen to music.
plural	We go to the library.	We do not (don't) go to the library.
	You drink beer.	You do not (don't) drink beer.
	They watch TV every night.	They do not (don't) watch TV every night.

Time expressions in present simple

always > often > usually > sometimes > seldom > never

e.g., David **always** eats with his mom. / Robert **often** does business with dangerous men. / We **usually** drive to work. / Olive **sometimes** tells jokes. / The Murrays **seldom** sit in the library. / David **never** goes to the gym.

every day / every week / every month / every year

e.g., Olive does different exercises **every day**. She jogs, swims, plays basketball, and does kickboxing.

Object pronouns

me, you, him, her, it, us, them

They know **me**. / It's **you**. / Jessica cooks for **him/her**. / They drink **it**. / She likes **us**. / She steals **them**.

Exercise 1 Change the following verbs into the third person singular forms.

1. run
2. work
3. do
4. watch
5. cry
6. enjoy

Exercise 2 Fill in the blanks with the correct object pronoun.

e.g., *I walk with my dog every day. = I walk with (it) every day.*

1. We helped our mother in the kitchen.

   = We helped (   ) in the kitchen.

2. They like my brother and me.

   = They like (   ).

3. Mike doesn't play with Sarah and Jerry.

   = Mike doesn't play with (   ).

Exercise 3 Change the sentences by following the directions.

e.g., *I watch TV in the morning. (+ usually)* → *I usually watch TV in the morning.*

1. She studies at a café. (+ always)

    → (   )

2. I buy coffee from vending machines. (+ often)

    → (   )

3. My father cooks at home. (+ never)

    → (   )

4. We watch a movie at a movie theater. (+ sometimes)

    → (   )

Exercise 4 Change the sentences into the positive or negative sentences.

e.g., *I study English. Negative: I do not (don't) study English.*

1. She listens to English radio programs.

    Negative: (   )

2. These machines work.

    Negative: (   )

3. He does not visit his uncle.

    Positive: (   )

4. They don't run this place.

    Positive: (   )

Speaking Activity

Exercise 1

Fill in the table with activities that you usually do. Exchange your information with your partner(s).

e.g., *I practice the piano on Mondays.*

Monday	*Practice the piano / ...*
Tuesday	
Wednesday	
Thursday	
Friday	
Saturday	
Sunday	

Exercise 2

Look at the list below. Circle the one that is true for you. Tell your answers to your partner(s).

e.g., *I live alone. I don't live with my family.*

I listen to pop music. I sometimes listen to classical music, too.

live alone	live with family
go to bed before midnight	go to bed after midnight
have a big family	have a small family
watch movies at home	watch movies at the cinema
listen to pop music	listen to classical music

Exercise 3

Tell your partner(s) how often you do the following activities. Add more information. Then ask your partner(s).

e.g., *I never miss the last train. I go home before nine. How about you?*

I sometimes miss the last train. I wait for the first train. How about you?

1. miss the last train
2. go to the gym
3. study in the library
4. go to karaoke
5. send text messages
6. eat at the school cafeteria

Role Play

CD: Track 12

Guest:	Hello, I have a room booked at your hotel.
Receptionist:	What's your name, please?
Guest:	I'm Sarah Jones.
Receptionist:	One moment, please. Oh yes, Ms Jones. Welcome to our hotel. Here is your key.
Guest:	Thank you.
Receptionist:	Is there anything else I can do for you?
Guest:	Yes. Do you have any sport facilities?
Receptionist:	Yes, we do. There is a swimming pool, a sauna, and a gym.
Guest:	What time are they open?
Receptionist:	All facilities are open from 9:00 a.m. till 9:30 p.m.
Guest:	What time is the restaurant open?
Receptionist:	We serve breakfast from 6:30 to 10:00. Lunch is from 12:00 to 4:00 and then the restaurant is open till 10:30.
Guest:	OK. Thank you for your help.
Receptionist:	My pleasure.

USEFUL EXPRESSIONS
IN CONVERSATION
What's your name, please?
One moment, please.
Here is ...
Is there anything else I can do for you?
What time are they open?
Thank you for your help.
My pleasure.

Homemade Soup and Wine

The target of this chapter is to understand:

・Questions in present simple with short answers（一般動詞現在形の疑問文）

・Verbs of preference + gerunds（動名詞を使った好みを示す表現）

Review Activity

次の表はメアリーの日常を表したものです。彼女の日常を英語で説明してみましょう。

(This is Mary's everyday activity. Explain her activities.)

e.g., *Mary gets up at 6:30.*

6:30 AM	get up
7:00 AM	breakfast
8:00 AM	go to university
12:00 PM	lunch
5:00 PM	part-time job
9:30 PM	go home
10:00 PM	dinner
11:00 PM	take a bath
12:00 AM	go to bed

Warm-Up

1. 料理はよくしますか？
2. 警察はどのような仕事をしていますか？

Let's Watch!

Scene 4-1

🔊 **CD: Track 13 / DVD: Chapter 09** (07:55-09:18)

 Words and Phrases

please: Please have a seat.

change: change into a T-shirt

supper: have pasta for supper

I'm fine.: Don't worry. I'm fine.

hungry: The dog is hungry.

darling: Hello, darling.

some: have some coffee

homemade: eat homemade bread for lunch

soup: eat/have soup

amazing: The actor is amazing!

tuck in: I made dinner. Tuck in!

Script of the Scene

Jessica: Here you are, Olive! Please change and come for ¹(   ).

Olive: I'm ²(   ), really. I'm not hungry.

Jessica: Yes, you are. Don't be silly, darling. ³(   ) some homemade ⁴(   ) on the table.

Olive: For ⁵(   )?

....

Jessica: Come and sit here, Olive.

Olive: Thank you. Wow, ⁶(   ) ⁷(   ) amazing.

Jessica: Thank you. Tuck in!

Words and Phrases

children: have two children

It's time to: It's time to wake up.

go to bed: go to bed at ten

stay: stay in the room

enjoy: enjoy lots of food

tricky: a tricky question

but then again ...:

   It's a bit strange, but then again, I'm interested.

Why not?: Have some more. – Why not?

Tell me: Tell me. Why are you in the UK?

anything: I don't know anything about art.

not even: It's not even funny!

pretty: a pretty girl

seem: His parents seem really nice.

awfully: I'm awfully sorry.

boring: a boring book

policeman: I want to be a policeman.

How many...?:

   How many brothers do you have?

criminal: a dangerous criminal

be wrong : Your answer is wrong.

solve: solve math problems

difficult: a difficult question

case: a murder case

stolen: a stolen car

bicycle: ride a bicycle

drunk driving:

   Don't even think about drunk driving.

lost: a lost child

serious: a serious face

matter: a personal matter

lose: lose money

community:

   Many people live in this community.

Script of the Scene

Jessica: Okay children, it's time for me to go to bed, but you two stay here and enjoy the
^{8}(   ).

David: More wine?

Olive: Wine is a ^{9}(   ) thing. But then again ... ^{10}(   )
^{11}(   )?

David: So, ^{12}(   ) ^{13}(   ). Why are you so ^{14}(   )
^{15}(   ) those old stones? They don't do anything! They're not even
pretty. Your job ^{16}(   ) awfully boring.

Olive: Why do you work as a policeman in Old Berry? How many criminals
^{17}(   ) you ^{18}(   ) in this town? Two?

David: You're so wrong! I ^{19}(   ) many difficult cases every day.

Olive: Stolen bicycles? Drunk driving? Lost cats?

David: Lost cats are a serious matter. Think of the children that lose them.

Olive: I'm so sorry. Yes, you do a great job for the ^{20}(   ).

Comprehension Check

Exercise 1 True (T) or false (F)?

1. (   ) Supper is ready for Olive.
2. (   ) The three people stay up late.
3. (   ) David is interested in the stone circles.
4. (   ) Olive and David drink beer.
5. (   ) Olive asks about David's job.
6. (   ) David works for the community.

Exercise 2 Answer the following questions.

1. Is David a policeman?   (   )
2. Has Olive got a room at the B&B?   (   )
3. Has David got a present for Olive?   (   )
4. Does David pour some wine for Olive? (   )
5. Who leaves the dinner table first?   (   )
6. What does Jessica make for supper? (   )

Exercise 3 Put the sentences in the correct order.

1. David explains his job.
2. Jessica invites Olive to dinner.
3. Jessica leaves.
4. Olive apologizes to David.
5. Olive comes back to the B&B.
6. They begin eating.

_____ → _____ → _____ → _____ → _____ → _____

Grammar

Questions in present simple

	questions	answers
singular	Do I steal paintings?	Yes, I do. No, I do not (don't).
	Do you like red wine?	Yes, you do. No, you don't.
	Does he/she/it listen to music?	Yes, he/she/it does. No, he/she/it does not (doesn't).
plural	Do we play soccer?	Yes, we do. No, we do not (don't).
	Do you play the piano?	Yes, you do. No, you do not (don't).
	Do they work for a community?	Yes, they do. No, they do not (don't).

Talking about preferences

love
like
don't mind
dislike   } + verb *-ing*
hate
enjoy
be interested in

I love driving.
You like dancing.
He doesn't mind cleaning.
She dislikes taking exams.
It hates taking a bath.
We enjoy going to club activities.
They are interested in taking photos.

Gerunds

- In general   → + ing

- For one syllable words: short vowel + consonant → double consonant + ing
  e.g., run → running / swim → swimming

- a verb ending in -e   → ~~e~~ + ing
  e.g., take → taking / drive → driving

- a verb ending in –y   → y + ing
  e.g., study → studying / play → playing

Exercise 1 Change the verbs into *-ing* forms.

1. eat
2. make
3. watch
4. chat
5. begin
6. drive
7. open
8. cut
9. stop
10. see
11. sit
12. listen

Exercise 2 Fill in the blanks.

1. A: (   ) she smoke?
   B: No, she (   ), but her father (   ).

2. A: (   ) you like classical music?
   B: Yes, my sister and I love (   ) to concerts.

3. A: (   ) you like (   ) coffee?
   B: No, I (   ). I always drink tea.

4. A: (   ) he enjoy (   ) the guitar?
   B: Yes, he (   ). He plays it every day.

Exercise 3 Change the sentences by following the directions.

e.g., *He likes drinking.* Question: *Does he like drinking?* Yes: *Yes, he does.*

1. She wants new shoes. Question: (   )
   Yes: (   )

2. They need money. Question: (   )
   Yes: (   )

3. It takes five minutes. Question: (   )
   No: (   )

4. The dog enjoys running outside.
   Question: (   )
   Yes: (   )

5. You like doing household chores.
   Question: (   )
   No: (   )

Speaking Activity

Exercise 1

Combine the words in column A with those in column B to make sentences that are true for you. Share your answers with your partner(s).

e.g., *I hate studying math.*

A	B
enjoy	study math
like	sing
love	read comic books
be interested in	play video games
dislike	chat with friends
hate	post pictures on SNS
	ride the train during rush hour
	watch horror movies
	give a presentation in class
	travel around the world

Exercise 2

Ask and answer the following questions with your partner(s).

1. When do you like traveling, in the summer or winter?

2. Which movies do you like watching, sci-fi or action?

3. What are you interested in doing in the future?

4. What do you hate doing in the morning?

5. What do you love doing with your friends?

6. What do you dislike eating?

Exercise 3

Take turns asking about the following people with your partner. Make four questions with *Does he/she...?*. Then ask your questions to your partner. If your partner's answer is correct, then he or she gets one point. The person with more points is the winner.

e.g., *Does she come from the U.S.?*   –*Yes, she does.*   (1 point)
                                       –*No, she doesn't.* (0 points)

     Does Olive live with Jessica?   –*No, she doesn't.* (1 point)
                                       –*Yes, she does.*   (0 points)

CD: Track 15

Kate: Hi, I'm glad you're home. I'm hungry. Is there something to eat?

Paul: Mom always leaves lunch for us in the microwave.

Kate: Sure, sure, I'm so hungry. I have to eat something right now.

Paul: There is spaghetti in the fridge. Can you find some dishes? I'll start microwaving.

Kate: Look at the sink. Everything is dirty.

Paul: Oops... Somebody has to wash it.

Kate: I hate washing up.

Paul: But you love eating. So, start washing.

Kate: Where is the dish soap?

Paul: It's probably next to the sink, as always. Check before you ask.

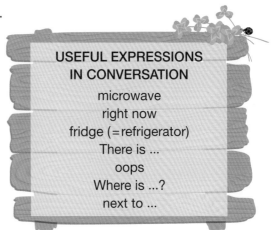

USEFUL EXPRESSIONS IN CONVERSATION
microwave
right now
fridge (=refrigerator)
There is ...
oops
Where is ...?
next to ...

[Chapter 5]

Jogging

The target of this chapter is to understand:

・*There is/are*（There構文）

・Prepositions of place（場所を表す前置詞）

・Definite article, indefinite articles, and no article（冠詞：不定冠詞，定冠詞，無冠詞）

Review Activity

ペアになって次の活動が好きかどうか英語で聞いてみましょう。

(Ask your partner(s) if they like doing the following activities.)

e.g., *Do you like playing the guitar? – Yes, I do, / No, I don't.*

Warm-Up

1. 健康のために何かしていますか？
2. あなたの街にはどんなものがありますか？

Let's Watch!

Scene 5-1

CD: Track 16 / DVD: Chapter 11 (10:48-11:22)

Words and Phrases

care for: Care for another one?

company: I enjoy your company.

jogger: joggers in the park

sort of: I sort of like singing.

as (preposition)**:** work as a teacher

police officer: His uncle is a police officer.

need to: I need to study for a test.

fit: My father is tall and fit.

show: show interest in art

Show me what you've got.:

  I hear you can sing. Show me what you've got.

Script of the Scene

David: Hi! ¹(   ) for some company?

Olive: You're a jogger then?

David: Yeah, ²(   ) ³(   ). As a ⁴(   )

  ⁵(   ), I need to stay fit.

Olive: All right, show me what you've ⁶(   ).

🔊 **CD: Track 17 / DVD: Chapter 12** (11:22-12:36)

 **Words and Phrases**

break: a 15-minute break

such: He is such a kind person.

lovely: lovely weather

everything: Everything is OK.

pub: drink beer at a pub

community center:
 visit the community center

swimming pool: go to the swimming pool

cinema: eat popcorn at a cinema

movie: watch a movie

interesting: This book is interesting.

opportunity: a good opportunity

know: I know some good restaurants.

a few: a few days

Look.: Look. I'm sorry about yesterday.

short: short hair

Would you like to...?:
 Would you like to drink something?

go out: go out for a walk

a drink: get a drink

🌿 **Script of the Scene**

Olive: Are you okay? [7](   ) you [8](   ) a break?

David: I'm ... okay ... but maybe [9](   ) water.

Olive: It's not [10](   ) [11](   ) bad town.

David: Come on, it's lovely! And [12](   ) everything here: [13](   ),
 a community center, a swimming pool, even a small cinema ...

Olive: Does it do 3D? You know, we Americans only watch 3D movies.

David: No, it [14](   ). But there are interesting things to do and even some
 business opportunities, too ... And some nice people ... [15](   )
 [16](   ) [17](   ) nice people in Old Berry.

Olive: Yeah, I know a few of them.

David: Look, I know you're only [18](   ) the town for a short time, but ...
 Would you like to [19](   ) [20](   ) for a drink with me?

🔊 **CD: Track 18 / DVD: Chapter 13** (12:36-12:59)

 **Words and Phrases**

idea: I have an idea.

finish: finish my homework

project: work on a big project

local: a local paper

history: study art history

about: I know nothing about you.

be ready for: Are you ready for your test?

jogging: Jogging is good for health.

🫒 Script of the Scene

Olive: David, it's not ²¹(   ) good ²²(   ). I need to finish my
project.

David: But I know everything about local history! ²³(   ) ²⁴(   )
with me is good for your project!

Olive: Is it? ... All right then! ... Are you ²⁵(   ) for some more jogging?

Comprehension Check

Exercise 1   **True (T) or false (F)?**

1.   (   ) There aren't many kind people in Old Berry.

2.   (   ) Olive agrees to go out with David.

3.   (   ) Olive is in Old Berry for a short time.

4.   (   ) David knows about the local history.

Exercise 2   **Answer the following questions.**

1.   Is there a swimming pool in Old Berry?   (   )

2.   Is there a 3D movie theater in Old Berry? (   )

3.   Are there job opportunities in Old Berry? (   )

4.   Are there many nice people in Old Berry? (   )

5.   Who runs faster, David or Olive?   (   )

6.   Why does Olive reject David?   (   )

Exercise 3   **Put the sentences in the correct order.**

1.   David asks her out again.

2.   David talks about Old Berry's good points.

3.   David wants something to drink.

4.   Olive talks about movie theaters in the US.

5.   Olive turns down David.

6.   Olive and David talk under a big tree.

_____ → _____ → _____ → _____ → _____ → _____

Grammar

There is ... / There are ...

positives	questions	answers
There is (There's) a book on the table.	Is there a book on the table?	Yes, there is. No, there is not (isn't).
There are (There're) books on the table.	Are there books on the table?	Yes, there are. No, there are not (aren't).

Prepositions of place

under, on, between, in, below, above, next to, behind, in front of

e.g., There is a suitcase under the bed. / Some pictures are on the wall. / There is a small lamp between the beds. / Her laptop is in the bag. / The sun sets below the horizon. / The sun rises above the horizon. / There is a flower next to the mirror. / The curtains are behind the chest. / Olive is in front of the window.

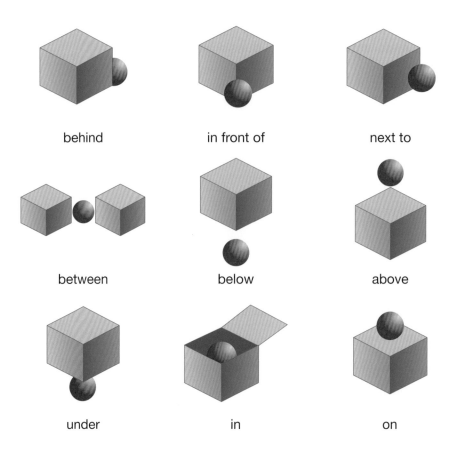

behind	in front of	next to
between	below	above
under	in	on

Articles

a/an → speaking of something for the first time:	
It's **an** old town. / He's **a** new client.	

the → speaking of something mentioned before:
It's not **a** bad town. Come on, **the** town is lovely.
→ speaking of something unique, one of a kind:
Where is **the** airport in Old Berry? (There is only one airport in Old Berry.)

no article (a/an/the)
→ before plural nouns: There are (a/an/the) pubs in Old Berry.
→ before uncountable nouns: There is water in the bottle.
→ before nationalities: We are (a/an/the) Americans and we only watch 3D movies.
→ before the names of towns and states: I live in (a/an/the) Old Berry.
Are you from (a/an/the) Poland?

Exercise 1 Fill in the blanks with the correct forms.

1. A: (   ) there a mail box around here?
   B: Yes, (   ) (   ). It's just over there.

2. A: (   ) there many tourists in the winter?
   B: No, (   ) (   ), but there (   ) many in the
   spring.

Exercise 2 Fill in the blanks with *a*, *an*, *the* or × (no article).

My name is (×   ) Gabriella Aguilar and I'm 26 years old. I live alone in
¹(   ) apartment in ²(   ) New York City. It's ³(   )
great city. I am ⁴(   ) art consultant. Now I am in ⁵(   ) small
town called ⁶(   ) Old Berry. I have to steal ⁷(   ) art painting.
⁸(   ) painting is ⁹(   ) masterpiece.

Exercise 3 Select items and locations to make questions with *Is / Are
there...?*, and answer the questions with *Yes* and *No*.

e.g., *Question → Is there a cat in the corner? Yes, there is / No, there isn't.*

Items: a convenience store, a park, many factories, students, flowers, a whiteboard
Locations: near here, in the neighborhood, in front of the classroom, on the campus,
in the garden

1. Question: (   )
   Yes: (   ) / No: (   )
2. Question: (   )
   Yes: (   ) / No: (   )
3. Question: (   )
   Yes: (   ) / No: (   )

Exercise 1

Try to make as many sentences as you can with *there is / there are* and prepositional phrases.

e.g., *There is a piece of paper next to the telephone.*

Useful expressions: tablet, notebook, between, next to

Useful expressions: a bowl of salad, a bottle of wine, plate, candle, flowers

Exercise 2

Draw a picture of your room in the space below. Explain your picture using *there is/ there are* and prepositions to your partner(s).

e.g., *There is a bed next to the desk. There is a clock above the desk.*

Role Play

((((CD: Track 19

Helen: Hi, Michael. I'm ready to go.

Michael: Great. Where would you like to go?

Helen: I'd like to see the nightlife in Yorkshire.

Michael: All right. Let's hit the town!

Helen: Great! What's the plan?

Michael: First, a restaurant, then a pub or a romantic walk.

Helen: It sounds nice but not very exciting. Do you have a plan B?

Michael: I want to show you the old town by night.

Helen: Oh, lovely! And then?

Michael: Would you like to watch a film?

Helen: Yeah, let's go to the movie theater.

USEFUL EXPRESSIONS
IN CONVERSATION

Let's hit the town.

What's the plan?

It sounds nice.

plan B

by night

lovely

In the Pub

The target of this chapter is to understand:

・*Be*-verb in past simple（be動詞の過去形）

・Past simple: regular and irregular verbs（規則変化動詞と不規則変化動詞の過去形）

・*Wh*-questions: *who, what, when, where, which*（wh疑問文）

・*Would like*（would likeを含む文）

Review Activity

写真を見て、何がどこにあるかthere is/areと前置詞を使って説明しましょう。

(Explain what you see with *there is/are* and prepositional phrases.)

e.g., *There is a mirror on the cupboard*.

Warm-Up

1. barとpub、居酒屋の違いを考えてみましょう。
2. パソコンでメールをよく送りますか？

Let's Watch!

Scene 6-1

CD: Track **20** / DVD: Chapter **14** (12:59-14:21)

Words and Phrases

one more: one more cup of tea

pint: two pints of beer

lager: Lager or wine?

whiskey: a whiskey and water

on the rocks: Straight or on the rocks?

pool: play pool

impress: impress the audience

put: put the dog in the cage

What can I say? :
  What can I say...it's not my fault.

deserve: She deserves the money.

talkative: I don't like talkative people.

adore: My parents adore small animals.

Script of the Scene

Barman: One more pint of lager and one more whiskey on the ¹(   ).

David: Not the pool! I ²(   ) ³(   ) how to impress you!

Bill: David, you are a lucky man. She's ⁴(   ).

David: Bill, weren't you ⁵(   ) ⁶(   )?

Bill: The prison you put me in.

David: ⁷(   ) can I say, Bill ... You deserved it.

Bill: ⁸(   ) your name, lovely girl? She's not very talkative, that's a good thing. I adore women like that! You don't meet many of them ⁹(   )
¹⁰(   ).

Words and Phrases

date: go on a date

no time for: There's no time for sleep.

loser: Don't call me a loser!

like (preposition): The cloud looks like a duck.

Script of the Scene

Olive: This date was [11]( ) bad [12]( ). I really need to finish my project now. I have no time for ...

David: A loser [13]( ) [14]( )?

Olive: Good night, David.

(Olive is typing): *Hi Curtis,*

My name's Olive and I'm an archaeology student from New York. I'm in Old Berry now and ...

Comprehension Check

Exercise 1 True (T) or false (F)?

1. ( ) Bill was in prison.
2. ( ) Olive was good at pool.
3. ( ) The barman served some juice.
4. ( ) Bill is angry at David.
5. ( ) David knew Bill.
6. ( ) Olive wrote an e-mail to David.

Exercise 2 Answer the following questions.

1. Where did Olive and David go? ( )
2. What did David order at the pub? ( )
3. Who did Olive and David meet at the pub? ( )
4. Which person hit Bill, David or Olive? ( )
5. When did Olive send an e-mail? ( )

Exercise 3 **Put the sentences in the correct order.**

1. Bill approached Olive.

2. David was upset.

3. David was impressed by Olive.

4. Olive attacked Bill.

5. Olive went back to her room.

6. The barman put two glasses on the counter.

_____ → _____ → _____ → _____ → _____ → _____

Grammar

Time expressions in past simple

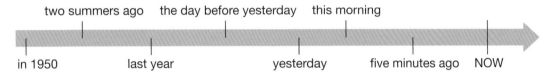

two summers ago   the day before yesterday   this morning

in 1950   last year   yesterday   five minutes ago   NOW

Be-verb in past simple

Present Simple	Past Simple
I am a university student now.	I was a university student then.
You are at home today.	You were at home last weekend.
Olive is in the UK these days.	Olive was in the USA last month.
Curtis is in a pub every Friday.	Curtis was in a pub last Friday.
Oh, it is a beautiful summer this year.	Oh, it was a beautiful summer last year.
We are in this park every morning.	We were in this park yesterday morning.
You are happy in Old Berry this summer.	You were happy in Old Berry last summer.
They are in their park now.	They were in their park three days ago.

Regular verbs in past simple

• In general	→ + ed
e.g., finish → finished / call	→ called
• ending in –e	→ + d
e.g., hope → hoped / solve	→ solved
• vowel + y	→ + ed
e.g., enjoy → enjoyed / stay	→ stayed
• vowel + consonant + y	→ **y** + ied
e.g., study → studied	
• short vowel + consonant	→ double consonant + ed
e.g., stop → stopped	

Irregular verbs in past simple

be	→ was / were	go	→ went	say	→ said
come	→ came	have	→ had	see	→ saw
do	→ did	know	→ knew	sleep	→ slept
drink	→ drank	meet	→ met	steal	→ stole
eat	→ ate	put	→ put	take	→ took
get	→ got	run	→ ran	tell	→ told

Wh-pronouns (*who, what, when, where, which*)

Who's that woman? – She is Olive.

Who came late? – David did.

What's her name? – She is Jessica.

What do you do in the evenings? – I always watch the news on TV.

When were you in New York? – I was there last winter.

When does she usually jog in the park? – Olive usually jogs in the morning.

Where is your phone? – It's in my bag, I think.

Where do you live? – I live in London.

Which is your bag, this one or that one? – That one.

Which car do you like, the blue or the red one? – I like the blue car.

Would like

Would you like to have dinner with us? – Yes. That's a good idea. Thank you.

Would you like something to eat? – Yes, please. Some soup, please.

Would you like a cup of coffee? – No, thank you.

Would you like some wine? – Wine is a tricky thing ... But yes, please.

Exercise 1 **Change the verbs into the past tense forms.**

1. enjoy
2. cry
3. bring
4. come
5. hit

6. eat
7. sing
8. go
9. have
10. arrive

11. drink
12. put
13. cut
14. sleep
15. buy

Exercise 2 **Fill in the blanks.**

1. A: Would you (   ) (   ) join us?

   B: Yes, I'd love to. Thank you.

2. A: Would you like some more bread?

   B: (   ), (   ) (   ). I'm full.

Exercise 3 **Change the sentences by following the directions.**

e.g., *You bought a book.   Question: What did you buy*?

1. Curtis got an e-mail.   Question: (Who   )

2. Olive bought a party dress.   Question: (What   )

3. They drank whiskey at the pub. Question: (What   )

4. She wanted a red or a blue dress. Question: (Which   )

5. David drove to London yesterday. Question: (When   )

6. He bought a nice suit at that store. Question: (Where   )

7. My mother was interested in learning French at university.
   Question: (When   )

8. Sarah and her friends enjoyed playing tennis.
   Question: (What   )

Speaking Activity

Exercise 1

Ask and answer the following questions with your partner(s).

1. What TV program did you watch last weekend?

2. What did you eat for breakfast this morning?

3. What were you interested in doing five years ago?

4. Where did you travel to last year?

5. When did you go to bed last night?

6. Which did you enjoy as a child, playing outdoors or indoors?

Exercise 2

Look at the pictures below. Explain what Olive and David did together with your partner(s).

Two nights ago...

Yesterday...

Later...

In the evening...

Exercise 3

This is a conversation between a bartender and a customer. Practice the conversation with your partner. Then practice the conversation again by changing the orders.

Snacks	Main	Drinks
olives	fish and chips	lager (½ pint / pint)
popcorn	hamburger and fries	wine (red / white)
nachos	hot dog	whiskey

Barman: Are you ready to order?

Customer: Yes, I would like a lager and a whiskey.

Barman: No problem. Would you like half a pint or a pint?

Customer: A pint, please.

Barman: Okay. And how would you like your whiskey?

Customer: I'd like it on the rocks.

Barman: Would you like anything to eat?

Customer: Yes. I would like nachos and some fish and chips.

Barman: Is that all?

Customer: Yes. That's all. Thank you.

Role Play

CD: Track 22

Waiter: Good evening, sir. How can I help you?

Client: I have a table booked here.

Waiter: Can I have your name, please?

Client: My name is John Smith.

Waiter: A moment, please. Yes, Mr Smith. Come with me, please. Can I take your order?

Client: What is the chef's specialty?

Waiter: It's tomato soup for the starter, steak with fries for the main course, and chocolate cake for the dessert.

Client: I'll just have the main course, please.

Waiter: All right. Would you like something to drink?

Client: Yes. A pint of lager, please.

Waiter: Of course, sir. Thank you for your order. I'll be back with you shortly.

USEFUL EXPRESSIONS IN CONVERSATION

How can I help you?
have a table booked
Can I have your name, please?
Can I take your order?
the chef's specialty
I'll be back with you shortly.

Review 1

1 **Let's practice *this / that* and possessive *'s*.**

Look at the following people. Work with your partner to find out who they are and what their relationships are.

e.g., Q: *Who is that?*

   A: *This is Olive. She is Jessica's guest.*

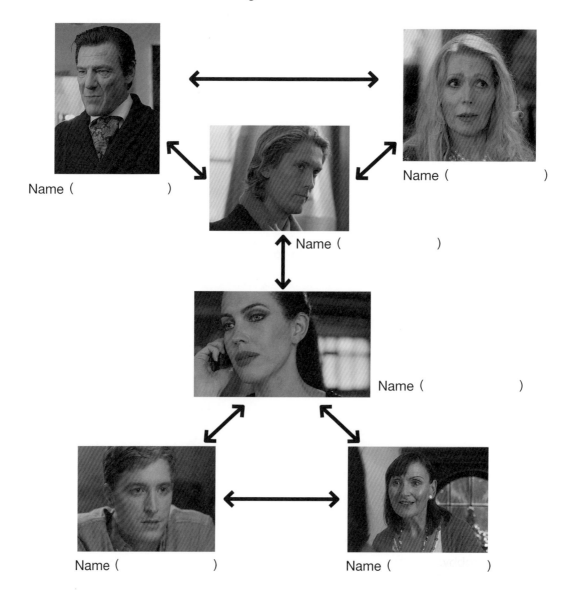

Name (   )

Name (   )

Name (   )

Name (   )

Name (   )

Name (   )

2 Let's practice making simple past and simple present sentences.

Look at what Mary did yesterday and what she does usually on weekdays. Explain her activities with your partner(s).

e.g., *She got up at 8:00 yesterday. She usually gets up at 6:30.*

	yesterday	regular activity
7:00 AM		get up
8:00 AM	get up	breakfast
8:30 AM	skip breakfast	go to university
9:30 AM	meet a friend	take the first class
12:00 PM	lunch at a restaurant	lunch at the cafeteria
3:00 PM	play pool	part-time job
4:45 PM	go home	
7:00 PM	dinner	go home
8:30 PM	write a report	dinner
12:00 AM	go to bed	go to bed

3 Let's practice making questions with *what*, *which*, *when*, and *where*.

Take turns interviewing each other using the table below.

· Partner A will be Sarah Jones. Partner B will be the interviewer. Sarah wants a part-time job at a restaurant.

· Partner B will be Jim Smith. Partner A will be the interviewer. Jim wants a part-time job at a language school.

e.g., A : What is your name?
       B : My name is Jim Smith.

	Job at a restaurant	Job at a language school
What	Name: Sarah Jones	Name: Jim Smith
How old	Age: 20	Age: 19
Where	From: England	From: Canada
Which	Job: to be a waiter or to be a cook	Job: to teach English or to teach French
When	Free: Mondays and Thursdays	Free: weekends
What	Hobby: play the piano	Hobby: watch movies

4 Let's practice saying your preferences by using preference verbs (e.g., *love* and *hate*) and *–ing* (gerund).

Ask and answer the following questions with your partner(s).

1. Which do you like, traveling alone or with your friends?

2. Which TV shows do you like watching, comedy or drama?

3. What are you interested in studying at university?

4. What do you hate doing at home?

5. What do you love doing in your free time?

6. What kind of books do you enjoy reading?

5 Let's practice making sentences with *there is/are* and prepositional phrases.

Work in pairs and take turns. Are there any of the following items in the classroom?

e.g., *Are there chairs in the classroom?*
    Yes, there are. There are chairs behind the desks.

Questions:	Items:	Locations:
Is there...? / Are there...?	blackboard, lectern, overhead projector, desk, chair, speaker, window, curtain, computer, fan, air conditioner, calendar, television, bookshelf, armchair, poster	under, on, between, in, near, above, next to, behind, in front of
Answers:		
There's... / There're...		
There isn't / There aren't		

6 Fill in the blanks.

Practice the role play with your partner.

CD: Track 23

Guest: Good morning. I'd like to book a room for one night, please.

Receptionist: ¹(   ) you like a single or a double room?

Guest: I'd like to book a single room, please.

Receptionist: OK, and ²(   ) you smoke?

Guest: No I don't. I would like a non-smoking room.

Receptionist: No problem. ³(   ) would you like to check in?

Guest: On Tuesday morning.

Receptionist: Okay. Can I help you with anything else?

Guest: Yes. ⁴(   ) you got a gym?

Receptionist: Yes, we have a 24-hour gym.

Guest: Great. Thank you.

[Chapter 8]

Thistle Flowers

The target of this chapter is to understand:

- Past simple: questions and short answers（過去形の疑問文と応答表現）
- Negatives in past simple（一般動詞過去形の否定文）
- Comparative and superlative of adjectives（形容詞を使った比較級と最上級）

Review Activity

メアリーは夏休みにハワイに行きました。何をしたのか英語で言ってみましょう。

(Mary went to Hawaii on her summer vacation. Describe what she did.)

e.g., *She arrived at Honolulu at 8:30.*

8:30 AM	arrive at Honolulu
11:30 AM	visit Diamond Head
1:30 PM	lunch
3:00 PM	check in to the hotel
3:30 PM	swim in the sea
5:30 PM	return to the hotel

Warm-Up

1. あなたにとって最も大切な物は何ですか？
2. 考古学とはどのような学問ですか？

CD: Track 24 / DVD: Chapter 16 (15:34-17:28)

Words and Phrases

dad: His dad has many paintings.

precious: a precious stone

let: She didn't let me in her room.

code: a secret code

enter: enter a building

smart: a smart child

call: We call him Mr Tanaka.

guest: We had many guests last night.

Why don't we ...?: Why don't we go for a drink?

Script of the Scene

Curtis: My dad keeps his precious paintings in that room – [1](   ) [2](   ) important thing in his life.

Olive: I'd love to see them!

Curtis: My father doesn't let anyone in! You need to know a special [3](   ) to enter the door.

Olive: But you're such a smart boy and you know the code.

Robert: Who's your [4](   ), Curtis?

Curtis: Dad, I thought you [5](   ) to London [6](   ).

Robert: I [7](   ). Robert Murray, but ... please call me Robert.

Olive: I'm Olive Green. Nice to meet you Mr Mur ... Robert.

Robert: So Curtis, you wanted to show your guest my paintings. All right, [8](   ) [9](   ) [10](   ) see them together?

 **Words and Phrases**

entertain: entertain children with stories

for a minute: wait for a minute

when: when I was young

stuff: There's a lot of stuff in the kitchen.

interest: This movie won't interest many people.

different from: My mother is different from me.

girlfriend: a pretty girlfriend

pretend: pretend to be rich

classy: a classy restaurant

vulgar: vulgar language

stupid: I was so stupid!

 **Script of the Scene**

Curtis: It's ¹¹( ). I need to ... er ...

Robert: You go and talk to her, son. Let me entertain your guest for a minute. "Thistle Flowers" ... ¹²( ) ¹³( ) work of Frederic Beaumont. Some people think he was the most ¹⁴( ) of the Impressionists. ¹⁵( ) you ¹⁶( ) that when he painted it in 1880 ...

Olive: ¹⁷( ). I study archeology. This stuff interests me.

Robert: Olive, you're very different from all Curtis's other ¹⁸( ). Most of them pretend to be classy and ¹⁹( ), but you pretend to be vulgar and ²⁰( ). Why do you do that?

 **Words and Phrases**

what you're talking about:

  I don't understand what you're talking about.

something: There's something I need to know.

deal with: deal with a problem

give ... a lift:

  He gave me a lift home last night.

information: collect information

Script of the Scene

Olive: I have ²¹( ) ²²( ) what you're talking about!

Robert: But I think you do, Ms Green.

Curtis: I'm sorry, Olive, there's something I need to deal with. Let me give you a lift into town, okay?

Olive: Yes, sure.

Robert: It's Murray. I need ²³( ) about a girl. She's American. Her name's Olive Green ...

Comprehension Check

Exercise 1 True (T) or false (F)?

1. (　) Campbell Manor's got a special room for art collections.
2. (　) Robert came back from London.
3. (　) Curtis told the special code to Olive.
4. (　) Olive met Robert for the first time.
5. (　) Curtis is only interested in smart women.
6. (　) Robert offered Olive a drive home.

Exercise 2 Answer the following questions.

1. Who is Robert?
(　　　　　　　　　　　　　　　　　　)
2. Did Robert go to London yesterday?
(　　　　　　　　　　　　　　　　　　)
3. Does Curtis know the special code to the room?
(　　　　　　　　　　　　　　　　　　)
4. What does Olive study?
(　　　　　　　　　　　　　　　　　　)
5. When did Beaumont paint "Thistle Flowers"?
(　　　　　　　　　　　　　　　　　　)
6. Does Robert want information about Olive?
(　　　　　　　　　　　　　　　　　　)

Exercise 3 Put the sentences in the correct order.

1. Curtis entered the room again.
2. Curtis got a phone call from his mother.
3. Curtis left the room.
4. Robert introduced himself to Olive.
5. Robert explained to Olive about "Thistle Flowers."
6. Robert requested information about Olive Green.

_____ → _____ → _____ → _____ → _____ → _____

Grammar

Positives / negatives / questions with *be*-verb in past simple

Positive:		I/he/she/it	was	in Jessica's B&B.
		you/we/they	were	
Negative:		I/he/she/it	was not (wasn't)	in that house.
		you/we/they	were not (weren't)	
Question:	Was	I/he/she/it		with Robert?
	Were	you/we/they		

Short answers: Were you in the library? – Yes, I was.

– No, I was not (wasn't).

Positives / negatives / questions in past simple

Positive:		I/you/he/she/it/we/they		arrived.
Negative:		I/you/he/she/it/we/they	did not (didn't)	run fast.
Question:	Did	I/you/he/she/it/we/they		drive a car?

Short answers: Did you watch it? – Yes, I did.

– No, I didn't.

Comparative of adjectives

- 1 syllable ➜ -er
  e.g., old ➜ older / small ➜ smaller
- 2 syllables + -y ➜ -ier
  e.g., funny ➜ funnier / pretty ➜ prettier
- short vowel + consonant ➜ double consonant + -er
  e.g., hot ➜ hotter / big ➜ bigger / sad ➜ sadder
- more than 2 syllables ➜ more + adjective
  e.g., boring ➜ more boring / important ➜ more important

Superlative of adjectives

- 1 syllable ➜ the + -est
  e.g., old ➜ the oldest / small ➜ the smallest
- 2 syllables + -y ➜ the + -iest
  e.g., funny ➜ the funniest / pretty ➜ the prettiest
- short vowel + consonant ➜ the + double consonant + -est
  e.g., hot ➜ the hottest / big ➜ the biggest / sad ➜ the saddest
- more than 2 syllables ➜ the most + adjective
  e.g., boring ➜ the most boring / important ➜ the most important

Exercise 1 Fill in the blanks with the correct form.

1. A: (   ) you out with anybody yesterday?

    B: No, we (   ). We were at home.

2. A: (   ) it snowy yesterday?

    B: Yes, (   ) (   ). It was very cold.

3. A: (   ) you check the weather forecast?

    B: No, I (   ). I was busy this morning.

4. A: (   ) she forget her student ID?

    B: Yes, she (   ). She went back home.

Exercise 2 Use the prompts and make questions with the past simple form. Give short answers.

e.g., *Olive / visit Tokyo two years ago*   *Question: Did Olive visit Tokyo two years ago?*

                                  Answers: Yes, she did. / No, she didn't.

1. she / be at her sister's yesterday

    Question: (   )

         Yes: (   )

2. Curtis / give his mother a call a little while ago

    Question: (   )

         No: (   )

3. they / be still students last summer

    Question: (   )

         Yes: (   )

4. you / finish your homework yesterday

    Question: (   )

         No: (   )

Exercise 3 Fill in the blanks with the comparative or superlative form of the word in brackets. Write your answers to the questions.

e.g., *Who is (the tallest) in your family? [tall]*
(My father is the tallest in my family.)

1. Which is (   ), Italian food or Thai food? [good]
(   )

2. What is (   ) thing in your house? [expensive]
(   )

3. Which is (   ), speaking or writing English? [difficult]
(   )

4. Which month is (   ) in Japan? [hot]
(   )

5. Where is (   ) place in the world? [pretty]
(   )

Speaking Activity

Exercise 1

Work in pairs. First, read the biographies of Mother Theresa and Isaac Newton.

Partner A: Make five questions about Mother Theresa (*Did she or Was she … ?*). Ask your questions to Partner B .

Partner B: Make five questions about Isaac Newton (*Did he or Was he … ?*). Ask your questions to Partner A.

Mother Theresa was a humanitarian. She helped the poor, the sick and the helpless. She studied English very hard in Ireland. In 1931, she became a nun. In 1979, she received the Nobel Peace Prize.

Isaac Newton was a scientist. He developed the theory of gravity. In university, he studied philosophy and astronomy. He later became a professor. In 1687, he published an important book about the three laws of motion.

Exercise 2.1

Look at the picture. Work with your partner(s). Compare Curtis and Olive. Decide who is:

old / tall / strong / intelligent / rich

e.g., *Curtis is richer than Olive.*

Exercise 2.2

Look at the pictures. Work with your partner(s). Compare New York, Okinawa, and Old Berry. Decide which of the three places is:

quiet / exciting / crowded / dangerous / polluted

e.g., *New York is the most polluted of the three.*

Role Play

CD: Track 27

Emma: It's my first time to visit a celebrity's mansion. Is it true that there are 10 bedrooms, a sauna, a swimming pool, and a library?

Beth: Don't forget about the cinema.

Emma: A cinema! Could I see it?

Beth: Of course. Right this way.

Emma: Wow! It's huge. And there are some films. I'd love to watch a movie!

Beth: Sure. Choose one.

Emma: What about *Roman Holiday* or *Mad Max*?

Beth: Let's watch *Mad Max*. It's more exciting and better.

USEFUL EXPRESSIONS
IN CONVERSATION
Could I ... ?
celebrity
sauna
Right this way.
huge
I'd love to ...

[**Chapter 9**]

Making the Plan

The target of this chapter is to understand:

・*Can*: ability and possibility（canを使った文：能力と可能性）
・Prepositions of movement（移動を示す前置詞）

Review Activity

ペアを組み、次に何が起こるか考えてみましょう。1-7 を並べ替え、文を過去形にして物語を続けましょう。
(Work with your partner(s). What do you think happens next? Continue the story by reordering the sentences 1-7. Change the sentences into the past tense form.)

Once upon a time, there was a humble woodcutter in a town. One day, he went out to the forest. He began cutting wood.

1. A god (come) out of the river with a golden ax and (ask) him, "Is this your ax?"
2. The god (give) the man both the golden ax and the silver ax.
3. The god (say), "You are very honest."
4. The man (give) the same answer, "No, it isn't."
5. The woodcutter (drop) his ax into the river by mistake.
6. The woodcutter (say), "No, it isn't." "That is not mine."
7. Then the god (show) him a silver ax and (ask) him, "Is this your ax?"

_____ → _____ → _____ → _____ → _____ → _____ → _____

Warm-Up

1. 得意なこと・不得意なことは何ですか？
2. どんな時に友達を遊びに誘いますか？

Let's Watch!

Scene 8-1

CD: Track 28 / DVD: Chapter 19 (19:06-19:59)

Words and Phrases

fence: put a fence in the yard

cut through: cut through a forest

climb: climb over the wall

perhaps:

   Perhaps you can talk to him about it.

hack: hack a computer

too: The man is too dangerous.

risky: This business is risky.

stream: fish in the stream

flow: This river flows across the town.

estate: a large estate with woods

Nope.: Have you got money? —Nope.

For Christ's sake!: Stop it for Christ's sake!

building: a high building

without: walk in the rain without an umbrella

more importantly:

   More importantly, he is honest.

escape: escape from the prison

Script of the Scene

Olive's monologue:

The fence ... that's easy. I can cut ¹(   ) it. I can climb ²(   ) it, but the cameras ...

Perhaps I can hack the cameras, but no ... That's too ³(   ) !

There's a stream flowing across the Campbell estate. There are no cameras there.

I can swim along it but ...

Nope! I'm no James Bond, for Christ's sake!

How ⁴(   ) I ⁵(   ) the building without anyone seeing me? And more importantly ...

How ⁶(   ) I ⁷(   ) the building and escape without anyone seeing me?

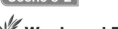
Words and Phrases

glad: I'm glad you came to my house.

be awake: He's not awake at this time.

still: She's still young.

tomorrow: There's a festival in town tomorrow.

charity: a charity concert

event: a social event

lots of:

    There are lots of interesting books in the room.

Poor you!:

    Poor you! You failed the exam?

hear: hear good news

make:

    A band can make the party more exciting.

fun: Jogging is fun for me.

Sure!: Would you like to come? – Sure!

Script of the Scene

Olive: Hi, Curtis. ^{8}(   ) ^{9}(   )?

Curtis: Hi, Olive. I'm glad you're still awake. Look, tomorrow in the evening there's a big ^{10}(   ) party at the Manor. A very ^{11}(   ) event, with lots of boring people coming.

Olive: ^{12}(   ) ^{13}(   ), I'm very sorry to hear that!

Curtis: ^{14}(   ) ^{15}(   ) like to go with me? You can ... make this thing more fun for me.

Olive: Sure! I'd ^{16}(   ) to come.

Comprehension Check

Exercise 1 True (T) or false (F)?

1. (   ) There are cameras along the stream.

2. (   ) It's safe to hack the cameras.

3. (   ) Curtis phoned her, but the line was busy.

4. (   ) Curtis is excited about the charity party.

5. (   ) Many people will join the party.

6. (   ) Olive accepted the invitation.

Exercise 2 Answer the following questions.

1. Where is the stream? ( )
2. Who talked to Olive on the phone? ( )
3. What is the purpose of the party? ( )
4. Can Olive go to the party? ( )
5. Which is more fun, going to the party alone or going with Olive?
   ( )

Exercise 3 Put the sentences in the correct order.

1. Olive thought about climbing the fence.
2. Curtis called Olive.
3. Curtis invited Olive to the party.
4. Curtis explained the party to Olive.
5. Olive thought about swimming down the river.

Grammar

Prepositions of movement

into, out of, around, away from, toward, past, onto, off, over, under, through, across, up, down

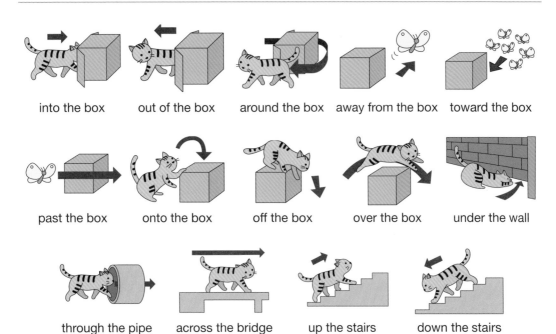

into the box	out of the box	around the box	away from the box	toward the box
past the box	onto the box	off the box	over the box	under the wall
through the pipe	across the bridge	up the stairs	down the stairs	

Can

→ **For things we are able to do**

My sister can play the piano.

A: Can they speak French?   B: Yes, they can. They are from Canada.

B: No, they can't. They can speak Spanish.

→ **For things it is possible to do**

Anything can happen.

A: Can you come to the party with me?   B: Yes, I can. Thank you for asking.

B: No, I can't. Maybe next time.

Positives / negatives / questions with *can*

Positive:		I/you/he/she/it/we/they	can	sing well.
Negative:		I/you/he/she/it/we/they	cannot (can't)	run fast.
Question:	Can	I/you/he/she/it/we/they		drive a car?

Short answers: Can you swim? – Yes, I can.
– No, I can't.

Exercise 1 **Fill in the blanks with the correct form.**

1. A: (   ) you fix the bike?

    B: No, I (   ). We need someone else.

2. A: (   ) this computer save lots of pictures?

    B: Yes, (   ) (   ). It's the latest model.

Exercise 2 **Select words and phrases from A and B to make sentences that are true for you.**

e.g., *I can (can't) swim across a 25-meter pool.*

A: jump, swim, run, walk, get, go	
B: over the lectern	on your hands
across a 25-meter pool	through a car window
up the stairs three steps at a time	around the campus in ten minutes

1. (   )
2. (   )
3. (   )
4. (   )
5. (   )
6. (   )

Speaking Activity

Activity 1

Look at the list below. Ask your partner if he/she can do the following activities. Answer and add more information.

e.g., *Can you play an instrument?*
     Yes, I can. I can play the ukulele.

1. play an instrument
2. drive a car
3. cook spaghetti
4. speak a second foreign language
5. do something creative
6. do a magic trick
7. do an impression
8. make funny faces

Look at the pictures and explain what happened with your partner(s).

e.g., *First, Olive got out of the car.*

Useful expressions: out of, car

1. Next, Curtis and Olive...

into, manor

2. Then Olive...

around, room

3. After that, Olive and Curtis...

along, statues

4. Suddenly, Robert...

behind, them

5. Finally, Olive...

across, room

Role Play

CD: Track 30

Carol: Hello! How are you today? How is your day?

Alfie: Hi, Carol. I'm fine, thanks, and you?

Carol: I'm OK, thank you. What are you up to these days?

Alfie: Well, I'm stuck at home.

Carol: What happened?

Alfie: Don't even ask.

Carol: Oh, come on. You can tell me. I won't laugh, I promise.

Alfie: I broke my leg.

Carol: Your leg? How did that happen?

Alfie: I climbed up the ladder to hang the curtains and ...

Carol: OK, OK, I don't want to know the rest! So I guess you are not coming to the concert tomorrow?

Alfie: No, no. I can go!

Carol: Can you? Really? With a broken leg? Oh, come on, don't be silly!

USEFUL EXPRESSIONS IN CONVERSATION

How is your day?

What are you up to?

I'm stuck at home.

Don't even ask.

come on

Don't be silly!

[Chapter 10]

Shopping for a Dress

The target of this chapter is to understand:

・Present continuous（現在進行形を含む文）

Review Activity

ペアを組み、下の絵の中から出来ること・出来ないことを交互に英語で伝えましょう。

(Work in pairs and take turns. Ask your partner whether he/she can/cannot do things below.)

e.g., *Can you ride a bike?*
Yes, I can. / No, I can't.

Warm-Up

1. 普段、洋服はどこで買いますか？
2. ダイエットはしたことがありますか？

Scene 9-1

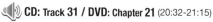 CD: Track **31** / DVD: Chapter **21** (20:32-21:15)

Words and Phrases

look for: look for an apartment

fancy: a fancy dress

mean: What does it mean?

formal: formal language

royal family:
  I've got a friend from the royal family.

sell: The shop sells organic foods.

kind: many kinds of products

evening dress:
  an evening dress for the party

buy: buy new shoes

Script of the Scene

Olive: I'm [1](   ) [2](   ) something fancy for a night out.

Shop assistant: Does a "night out" mean going to the pub?

Olive: No, it means going to a [3](   ) dinner with the friends of the royal family.

Shop assistant: Hm, I see ... Well then, this shop is the perfect place for you. We sell all [4](   ) [5](   ) evening dresses.

Olive: Oh, you do?

Shop assistant: No, we [6](   ). Women don't buy evening dresses in Old Berry. Sorry.

Words and Phrases

for some reason:
  For some reason, I thought about my family.

believe: I believe her story.

Shall we...?: Shall we go to school together?

try to: I'm trying to make new friends.

lose weight: She lost some weight.

say to oneself:
  He said to himself, "I'm so tired."

slim: I want to be slim like her.

enough to: I'm not old enough to drink.

as (conjunction): as you know

I'll take it.: I love it. I'll take it.

Script of the Scene

Olive: For some reason, I don't believe you. Shall we look for [7](   ) nice together?

....

Olive: That looks ... [8](   ). Why didn't you tell me you had it?

Shop assistant: Look, [9](   ) [10](   ) to lose [11](   ). Every day I look at this dress and I say to myself "I want to be slim enough to wear it!" But as you can see ...

Olive: I'll [12](   ) [13](   ).

Words and Phrases

excited: I'm so excited to see him.

ride: have a nice ride to the sea

Script of the Scene

Olive: Hey, Curtis.

Curtis: Hi, Olive. How are you?

Olive: I'm good. I'm [14](   ) for tonight.

Curtis: Are you?

Olive: Yeah. Nice [15](   ).

Curtis: Thank you. You look very beautiful.

Olive: Thank you.

Curtis: Can I take your bag?

Olive: Oh, no. I'm fine, thanks. Let's go.

Curtis: Yeah. Let's go.

Comprehension Check

Exercise 1 True (T) or false (F)?

1. (   ) Olive is going to a formal party.
2. (   ) David went into Olive's room.
3. (   ) The shop assistant didn't find a dress for Olive.
4. (   ) The shop assistant is on a diet.
5. (   ) Olive and Curtis are walking to the party.

Exercise 2 Answer the following questions.

1. Where did Olive go?   (   )
2. What was Olive looking for?   (   )
3. Why did Olive need a dress?   (   )
4. Why did the shop assistant want to lose weight?
    (   )
5. What was David doing in Olive's room? (   )

Exercise 3 Put the sentences in the correct order.

1. David found Olive's laptop.
2. Olive asked the shop assistant for help.
3. Olive decided to buy the dress.
4. Olive went into a clothes shop.
5. The shop assistant lied to Olive.
6. The shop assistant showed Olive a nice dress.

_____ → _____ → _____ → _____ → _____ → _____

Present continuous

→ **For current activities that are taking place at the moment of speaking**

Good morning. I'm looking for a dress.

It's raining outside. Don't go out.

Olive, come and sit with us. We're having a lovely dinner.

→ **For current activities that differ from the routine**

Curtis's parents usually don't work together, but they are working together these days. They are planning a charity event.

Olive doesn't read a lot about archaeology, but lately she is reading many books about the stone circles.

→ **For planned activities or actions in the near future**

Olive is leaving Old Berry next Friday.

Curtis is seeing Olive tonight.

Positives/negatives/questions with the present continuous form

Positive:	I	am (I'm)	walking outside.
	He/She/It	is ('s)	
	We/You/They	are ('re)	
Negative:	I	am not (I'm not)	eating a meal.
	He/She/It	is not (isn't)	
	We/You/They	are not (aren't)	
Question:	Am	I	sleeping?
	Is	he/she/it	
	Are	you/we/they	

Short answers: Is she studying? – Yes, she is.

– No, she isn't.

State verbs

want, like, hate, need, believe, know, see, smell, have, belong to, resemble

She likes Old Berry.	✕ She is liking Old Berry.
Beatrice loves gardening.	✕ Beatrice is loving gardening.
Mice hate cats.	✕ Mice are hating cats.
I believe in you.	✕ I am believing in you.

Exercise 1 Fill in the blanks with the correct form.

1. A: Can you help me move this stuff?
   B: Sorry, I can't. (   ) carrying luggage now.
2. A: What time (   ) this plane leaving?
   B: (   ) (   ) in 30 minutes.
3. A: (   ) they preparing for the exam?
   B: Yes, (   ) (   ). They are very nervous.
4. A: (   ) your brother still eating healthily?
   B: No, (   ) (   ). He quit his diet.

Exercise 2 Use the prompts and make sentences with the present continuous form.

e.g., *they / play baseball* → *They are playing baseball.*

1. you / write a report   (   )
2. the car / run at a high speed (   )
3. I / make pancakes   (   )
4. we / leave Narita Airport tonight (   )

Exercise 3 Use the prompts and make questions with the present continuous form. Then write the short answers.

e.g., *they / play basketball* → *Are they playing basketball? Yes, they are. / No, they aren't.*

1. your teacher / write on a whiteboard
   Question: (   )
      Yes: (   ) / No: (   )
2. your parents / go to work today
   Question: (   )
      Yes: (   ) / No: (   )
3. you / take a test right now
   Question: (   )
      Yes: (   ) / No: (   )

Speaking Activity

Exercise 1

Use the prompts and make questions with the present continuous form. Take turns asking and answering the questions.

e.g., *Is the teacher wearing a white shirt?*
Yes, she is. / No, she isn't. She is wearing a blue dress.

1. teacher / wear a white shirt
2. your mother / work in the office
3. it / rain outside
4. your family / go on vacation soon
5. you / eat out tonight
6. you / study hard for something

Exercise 2

Work with your partner(s). Look at the pictures and make as many sentences as you can with the present continuous form.

e.g., *The bartender is serving beer.*

Useful expressions: Olive, David, bartender, man in the green T-shirt, customer next to David, pool, beer

Useful expressions: Olive, David, Jessica, soup, bread, wine

Role Play

CD: Track 34

Shop assistant: Hello. Can I help you?

Customer: Yes, I'm looking for *Harry Potter*.

Shop assistant: But this is not a bookshop! It's a newsstand. We sell newspapers, magazines, tissues, phone cards ...

Customer: Oh, I'm sorry.

Shop assistant: That's OK. I'll tell you where the bookshop is. Can you see the bakery?

Customer: Yes, I can.

Shop assistant: The bookshop is opposite the bakery.

Customer: Oh yes, I can see it now.

Shop assistant: That's right. Have a nice day!

USEFUL EXPRESSIONS IN CONVERSATION

Can I help you?
I'm looking for ...
newsstand
opposite
Have a nice day!

Party Time

The target of this chapter is to understand:

・*Will*: future（willを使った文：未来）

Review Activity

ペアを組み、写真の人物が何をしているのか英語で言ってみましょう。

(Work in pairs. Explain what the people in the pictures are doing?)

e.g., *She is calling her client.*

1.

2.

3.

4.

5.

6.

Warm-Up

1. パーティー（誕生日会、成人式、結婚式など）に参加したことはありますか？
2. 初対面の人とはどのような会話をしますか？

Scene 10-1

CD: Track 35 / DVD: Chapter 24 (23:02-23:37)

Words and Phrases

Meet ...: Ken, this is Emi. Emi, meet Ken.

fetch: Can you go and fetch the paper for me?

Script of the Scene

Curtis: This is Olive. Olive, [1](   ) Beatrice.

Olive: [2](   ) you [3](   ) your mum [4](   ) to drink?

Curtis: Yeah, of course. Are you okay? All right?

Beatrice: Thank you. Yeah.

Scene 10-2

CD: Track 36 / DVD: Chapter 25 (23:37-24:58)

Words and Phrases

attract: attract many tourists

type: different types of people

first: the first man to walk on the moon

broken heart: cure the broken heart

beloved: my beloved wife

go away: Go away. I don't have time for you.

guess: I guess the story is true.

better: I know him better than you.

Script of the Scene

Beatrice: You know, Olive, my son attracts [5](   ) types of women. The first type of women are even [6](   ) stupid than he is. He leaves them with broken hearts. The other type are [7](   ) than Curtis and usually want to use him for our money. My ... beloved husband is very good at making them go away! But you ... My husband is [8](   ) [9](   ) you. So, I guess, that makes you even smarter than he thinks you are. Olive, my husband [10](   ) [11](   ) make you happy. His money will not make you happy. I know that [12](   ) than anyone.

....

Curtis: Are you OK?

....

Curtis: What was that about?

....

Curtis: Cheers.

Words and Phrases

Damn it!: Damn it! The car won't start!

give one's regards:
Give my best regards to your family.

Script of the Scene

Olive: Damn it, such a pretty dress! ... I'm ¹³(   ) ¹⁴(   ), Curtis. Give my regards to your mother.

Comprehension Check

Exercise 1 True (T) or false (F)?

1. (   ) Some of Curtis's ex-girlfriends are smarter than he is.

2. (   ) Beatrice is happy to be Robert's wife.

3. (   ) Olive changed her clothes.

4. (   ) Curtis introduced Olive and Beatrice to each other.

5. (   ) Olive met Beatrice for the first time.

6. (   ) Olive hit Curtis with a telephone.

Exercise 2 Answer the following questions.

1. What was the color of Olive's dress? (   )
2. Who did Olive meet at the party? (   )
3. What did Beatrice say to Olive? (   )
4. What did Olive put into Curtis's glass? (   )
5. Who brought Curtis to the bedroom? (   )

Exercise 3 Put the sentences in the correct order.

1. Beatrice introduced his mother to Olive.
2. Beatrice warned Olive.
3. Curtis got Beatrice something to drink.
4. Olive hit Curtis.
5. Olive drugged David.
6. Olive hid her dress.

_____ → _____ → _____ → _____ → _____ → _____

Will

→ **For things in the future**

All the guests will notice Olive at the party tomorrow.

Robert's money will not (won't) make Olive happy.

Will Olive's plan work? We will (we'll) see soon.

Will Olive be in Old Berry next year?   Yes, she will. She loves the town.

No, she will not (won't). She will (She'll) be in another country.

Positives / negatives / questions with *will*

Positive:		I / you / he / she / it / we / they	will ('ll)	go for a walk later.
Negative:		I / you / he / she / it / we / they	will not (won't)	exercise tonight.
Question:	Will	I / you / he / she / it / we / they		take a nap today?

Short answers: Will you come? – Yes, I will.

– No, I won't.

Future time expressions

in a few hours, tomorrow, next week, next month, next year, in 2035

The concert will begin in a few hours. / I'll see you tomorrow. / She will leave London next week. / We will have a long vacation next month. / Our school will hold a game next year. / My son will be 20 in 2035.

Exercise 1 **Fill in the blanks with the correct form.**

1. A: Will you buy this T-shirt?

   B: No, (   ) (   ). I don't like the color.

2. A: Will her father like her new boyfriend?

   B: Sure, (   ) (   ). He's kind and polite.

3. A: What (   ) happen next?

   B: You (   ) find out soon.

4. A: Who (   ) drive me to the station tomorrow?

   B: Your mother (   ). I'm busy tomorrow.

Exercise 2 Use the prompts and make positive and negative sentences with *will*.

e.g., *it / rain tomorrow*   Positive: *It'll (It will) rain tomorrow.*
                                           Negative: *It won't (will not) rain tomorrow.*

1. they / go to Kyoto next month

    Positive: (   )

2. I / call you back later

    Positive: (   )

3. you / join the party

    Positive: (   )

4. Olive / steal the painting tomorrow

    Negative: (   )

5. Curtis / get a job soon

    Negative: (   )

Exercise 3 Use the prompts and make questions with *will*.

e.g., *you / study Chinese next year* → *Will you study Chinese?*

1. we / have a meeting tomorrow

    (   )

2. the train / come in five minutes

    (   )

3. it / be hot this summer

    (   )

4. Olive and Curtis / go out for a drink tonight

    (   )

Speaking Activity

Exercise 1

Make questions with the following prompts. Take turns asking and answering the questions with your partner(s).

e.g., *you / go on vacation soon*

Will you go on vacation soon?   Yes, I will. I'll go to Bangkok with my family.

No, I won't. I'm too busy.

1. money / make a person happy

2. the population of Japan / continue to go down

3. the temperature / go up

4. you / live in a foreign country in the future

5. you / start a new hobby this year

6. you / go out with friends this weekend

Exercise 2

Work in pairs. Ask your partner what he/she will do tomorrow. Fill in the table with his/ her activities.

e.g., *What will you do at nine in the morning tomorrow?*

I will take an English class.

	Your partner's activities
9:00 AM	*English class*
12:00 PM	
3:00 PM	
6:00 PM	
9:00 PM	
12:00 AM	

Exercise 3

In your next class, you will watch the following scenes. Look at the pictures and guess what will happen with your partner(s).

1.

2.

3.

4.

5.

6.

Role Play

Christy: Hi. What's up? Oh, you look a bit worried.

Tomoki: Hi. I'm not worried. I just feel sick.

Christy: Yeah, you look terrible.

Tomoki: Well, thank you very much.

Christy: What's wrong?

Tomoki: I've got a cough and a runny nose.

Christy: Have you got a high temperature?

Tomoki: No, but I've got a headache, too.

Christy: I'm sorry to hear that. Have you got medicine?

Tomoki: No, I don't.

Christy: Here, I've got some. Take these and in two days you'll be fine.

Tomoki: Thanks, Christy.

USEFUL EXPRESSIONS IN CONVERSATION

What's up?

feel sick

look terrible

a runny nose

a high temperature

I'm sorry to hear that.

It's Time to Steal

The target of this chapter is to understand:

・Present perfect（現在完了を含む文）

・Past participle: regular and irregular verbs（規則変化動詞と不規則変化動詞の過去分詞）

・Imperative（命令文）

Review Activity

次の表はアンナの明日の予定を表したものです。英語で説明してみましょう。

(This is Anna's schedule for tomorrow. Describe what she will do tomorrow.)

e.g., *She'll take the train to Shinjuku at 11:45.*

11:45 AM	train to Shinjuku
12:30 PM	lunch with her friend
2:00 PM	cinema
4:15 PM	shopping at department stores
6:30 PM	home
7:00 PM	bath

Warm-Up

1. 盗まれたくない高価なものはありますか？
2. 人生最大の危機は何でしたか？

Let's Watch!

Scene 11-1

 CD: Track 39 / DVD: Chapter 27 (26:35-28:31)

Words and Phrases

unlock: unlock the door with a key

plan: a new plan

be out of one's mind:

She was out of her mind to leave him.

behind: hide behind the door

safe deposit box:

put gold in the safe deposit box

break into: break into the bank

document: read a document

agree on: agree on signing the document

current: This is current news.

address:

Tell me your address and phone number.

be out of one's reach:

Any dangerous items are out of his reach now.

kill: kill a mosquito

put ... in a good mood:

The food put the couple in a good mood.

Script of the Scene

Olive: [1]( ) unlocked the door. I'm in.

....

Olive: I'm looking at the painting [2]( ) [3]( ). Okay, let me just ...

Client: Olive, stop! The plan [4]( ) [5]( ).

Olive: What? Are you out of your mind?

Client: [6]( ) the painting there is a [7]( ) [8]( ) box. I want you to break [9]( ) it and take the documents that are inside.

Olive: We've agreed on something else! There is no time!

Client: Do it or [10]( ) [11]( ) Kirsch your mother's current address in San Fernando, [12]( ). You're out of his reach now but maybe killing your mum will put him in a better mood.

❧ Words and Phrases

yet: I haven't finished my homework yet.   **handcuffs:** put handcuffs on the criminal

be glad: I'm glad you like it.   **shoot:** shoot a tree with a gun

❧ Script of the Scene

Guy: She ^{13}(   ) ^{14}(   ) the painting!

....

Robert: Olive, ^{15}(   ) so ^{16}(   ) you haven't left the party

^{17}(   ). ... Guy, the handcuffs!

....

Robert: Stop, or I'll shoot you!

Comprehension Check

Exercise 1 True (T) or false (F)?

1. (   ) The door to "Thistle Flowers"   4. (   ) The client threatened Olive.
   was locked.   5. (   ) Olive's mother lives in Boston.
2. (   ) Olive stole "Thistle Flowers."   6. (   ) Robert shot Olive.
3. (   ) The plan has changed.

Exercise 2 Answer the following questions.

1. Where was the safe deposit box?   (   )
2. Who was Olive talking to on the phone? (   )
3. What is the new plan?   (   )
4. Why did Robert get angry?   (   )
5. What was Robert holding in his hand?   (   )

Exercise 3 Put the sentences in the correct order.

1. Olive entered Robert's art collection   4. Robert's guards attacked Olive.
   room.   5. The client suddenly changed the plan.
2. Olive stole important documents.   6. The client threatened Olive.
3. Robert pointed the gun at Olive.

_____ → _____ → _____ → _____ → _____ → _____

Present perfect

→ **An action or situation that started in the past and continues in the present**

Olive's (Olive has) **been** in Old Berry for a week.

I've **lived** in Tokyo since 1990.

Has David **been** a policeman for a long time?

– Yes, he **has**. He's **been** a police officer since 2012.

– No, he **hasn't**. He became a police officer last year.

→ **An action that was completed very recently**

I've **unlocked** the door. I'm in.

We've just **finished** work. I'm so tired.

Has the Black Friday sale **started**? – Yes, it **has**. It's (It has) just **started** today!

– No, it **hasn't**. I think it's (it is) tomorrow.

→ **An experience in an unspecified period between the past and the present**

They **haven't seen** this film yet.

Haruki Murakami **has written** many novels in his career.

Have you **visited** countries in Europe? – Yes, I **have**. I've **visited** most of them.

– No, I **haven't**. I've never **traveled** to Europe.

Positives/negatives/questions with the present perfect form

Positive:	I/You/We/They	have ('ve)	been to a hospital.
	He/She/It	has ('s)	
Negative:	I/You/We/They	have not (haven't)	visited Okinawa.
	He/She/It	has not (hasn't)	
Question:	Have	I/you/we/they	won a prize?
	Has	he/she/it	

Short answers: Have they come? – Yes, they have.

– No, they haven't.

Time expressions in present perfect

since May / since Christmas / since 2011	today / this week / this month / this year
for two days / for a week / for a year	never / yet (in negatives)
once / twice / three times	yet / ever (in questions)
lately / recently/ already / just	

Regular verbs in present perfect

- In general   → + ed
  e.g., finish → finished / call → called

- ending in –e   → + d
  e.g., hope → hoped / solve → solved

- vowel + y   → + ed
  e.g., enjoy → enjoyed / stay → stayed

- vowel + consonant + y   → **y** + ied
  e.g., study → studied

- short vowel + consonant   → double consonant + ed
  e.g., stop → stopped

Irregular verbs in present perfect

be → been	drive → driven	have → had
buy → bought	fight → fought	sell → sold
cut → cut	get → got / gotten	sing → sung

Imperative

Clean your room, please.
Call me later.
Stop, or I'll shoot you!

Please, don't worry.
Don't be sad.
Do not listen to him!

Exercise 1 Change the verbs into the past participle.

1. come
2. go
3. eat
4. have
5. steal

6. run
7. take
8. see
9. be
10. dream

11. lie
12. lay
13. write
14. put
15. give

Exercise 2 **Use the prompts and make sentences with the present perfect form.**

e.g., *Olive / see Curtis today* → *Olive has seen Curtis today.*

1. we / live here for 15 years (   )
2. I / just watch today's news (   )
3. she / be my best friend since university

   (   )

Exercise 3 **Use the prompts and make negative sentences with the present perfect form.**

e.g., *Curtis / play pool recently* → *Curtis has not played pool recently.*

1. I / spend lots of money   (   )
2. he / be never to Old Berry (   )
3. it / rain lately   (   )

Exercise 4 **Use the prompts and make questions with the present perfect form. Then write the short answers.**

e.g., *you / meet Jane since Christmas* → *Have you met Jane since Christmas?*
                                          Yes, I have. / No, I haven't.

1. we / know each other for five years
   Question: (   )
        No: (   )
2. you / already finish the homework
   Question: (   )
       Yes: (   )
3. May and Jeff / be a couple for 20 years
   Question: (   )
       Yes: (   )

Exercise 5 **Change the sentences by following the directions.**

e.g., *Turn down the volume! Negative: Do not (Don't) turn down the volume!*
      Don't open the door! Positive: Open the door!

1. Hold it tight!   Negative: (   )
2. Believe him!   Negative: (   )
3. Do not leave it alone!   Positive: (   )
4. Don't turn on the computer! Positive: (   )

Exercise 6 Select the words and phrases from A and B to make sentences that are true for you.

e,g., I have traveled abroad three times.

| A: send an e-mail, be on a diet, travel abroad, go to a concert, ride a train |

B: today	... times (e.g., three times)
this ... (e.g., this week)	lately
since ... (e.g., since last year)	yet
for ... (e.g., for two days)	never

1. ( )
2. ( )
3. ( )
4. ( )
5. ( )

Speaking Activity

Exercise 1

Combine the words in column A with those in column B to make questions. Take turns asking and answering each other.

e.g., Have you ever traveled abroad? – Yes, I have. I've been to Canada and Taiwan.
– No, I haven't. I'll travel to Greece next year.

A	B
travel	for a long time
read an interesting book	this month
go to Disneyland	this year
sing at karaoke	since high school
host a home party	lately
fail an exam	recently
go out on a date	never
study in the library	ever
live with your parents	yet

Exercise 2

Let's play "Simon Says!"

(i)   Make a group of three or more people.

(ii) Choose one person to be the leader.

(iii) The leader will give instructions to the other members of the group.

   (a) If the leader says "Simon says..." then the other members must do as the leader says.

   (b) If the leader does not say "Simon says..." then the other members must not do as the leader says.

Useful expressions:

Close your eyes.	Clap your hands twice.
Touch your shoulders.	Stand up.
Stomp your feet.	Sit down.

 Role Play

CD: Track 41

Boss: As far as I can remember, the painting exhibition takes place in June and the concert in July.

Assistant: Yes, that's correct.

Boss: Let's take care of the exhibition first.

Assistant: And what are we exhibiting—the paintings or the sculptures? Have you decided yet?

Boss: Yes, I have. We are going to do the sculpture exhibition.

Assistant: So what's next?

Boss: Set up a meeting with the artists.

Assistant: What will be the subject of this meeting?

Boss: Good question. Prepare the agenda first.

Assistant: All right. Will do.

USEFUL EXPRESSIONS
IN CONVERSATION
As far as I can remember
exhibition
sculpture
take place
take care of
set up
agenda
Will do.

Run!

The target of this chapter is to understand:

- *Have to*: obligation（have toを使った文：義務）
- *Can't*: prohibition（can'tを使った文：禁止）
- *Must*: obligation and recommendation（mustを使った文：義務と推薦）

Review Activity

ペアを組み、次の質問に英語で答えましょう。
(Work in pairs and take turns. Ask and answer the following questions with your partner.)

1. Where do you live? Have you lived there for a long time?
2. Have you ever been abroad? Where did you go?
3. Have you done extreme sports such as bungee jumping? What did you do?
4. Have you ever eaten anything strange? What did you eat?

Warm-Up

1. 人に嘘をついたことはありますか？どんな嘘でしたか？
2. 恋と仕事、どちらが大切だと思いますか？

Scene 12-1

CD: Track **42** / DVD: Chapter **29** (30:01-30:44)

Words and Phrases

pity:

It's a pity I can't see you anymore.

drop: I dropped my pen.

gun: You cannot use guns in Japan.

constable: a police constable

arrest: arrest two people for murder

employee: hire an employee

drug: drug an animal to make it sleep

Script of the Scene

Robert: Such a pity, Olive. I wanted us to be good friends.

David: ¹( ) your gun!

Robert: Constable Owen, you ²( ) ³( ) arrest this woman!
She's ⁴( ) ⁵( ) some very important business documents.

David: Mr Murray, you have to ⁶( ) your gun! Now!

Robert: She is a dangerous criminal! She attacked my employees and she
⁷( ) my son.

David: Olive, did you?

🌿 Words and Phrases

report: report the game result

must: You must go to the police.

calm down: Calm down a little bit.

Who the hell ...?:

   Who the hell broke my watch?

goddamn: Where is my goddamn pencil!?

work of art: collect many works of art

hurt: Her dog doesn't hurt people.

never: I never drive my family car.

The problem is...:

   The problem is…we don't have much money.

🌿 Script of the Scene

David: We have to report this! What we did … I ⁸(   ) ⁹(   ) things like that! I'm a policeman!

Olive: David, you must calm down!

David: Olive, who the hell are you? Is your name ¹⁰(   ) Olive? Are you really a criminal?

Olive: Where is your goddam car! Yes, David, I'm a criminal. I steal works of art. ¹¹(   ) I ¹²(   ) people, but I ¹³(   ) ¹⁴(   ) them.

David: ¹⁵(   ) ¹⁶(   ) me? What was my job in your plan?

Olive: The problem is I like you, David. ¹⁷(   ) ¹⁸(   ) I've liked anyone ¹⁹(   ) ²⁰(   ) ²¹(   ) time. So I didn't want to make trouble for you.

Comprehension Check

Exercise 1 True (T) or false (F)?

1. (   ) Olive told David the truth about her job.

2. (   ) Olive has murdered people.

3. (   ) Robert ordered David to arrest Olive.

4. (   ) Olive didn't find David's car key.

5. (   ) Olive drugged David.

Exercise 2 Answer the following questions.

1. Has Olive stolen "Thistle Flowers"? ( )
2. Has David already reported Olive's crime? ( )
3. Has Olive ever stolen works of art? ( )
4. Has Olive ever hurt anyone? ( )

Exercise 3 Put the sentences in the correct order.

1. David found Olive and Robert.
2. David found out about Olive.
3. Olive and David escaped.
4. Olive hit Robert with a flashlight.
5. Olive kissed David.
6. Olive left David and ran away.

_____ → _____ → _____ → _____ → _____ → _____

Have to / has to

→ For things that we are obliged to do

You **have to** sign your name here.

She didn't sleep much last night, but she **has to** get up now, or she'll be late.

Mom, **do I have to** brush my teeth? — Yes, you **do**. You ate some chocolate.

Do we **have to** finish this project by tomorrow? — No, you **don't**. It's due next week.

Positives/negatives/questions with _have to / has to_:

Positive:		I/You/We/They	have to	lock the door.
		He/She/It	has to	
Negative:		I/You/We/They	do not (don't) have to	go home tonight.
		He/She/It	does not (doesn't) have to	
Question:	Do	I/you/we/they	have to	wake up early?
	Does	he/she/it	have to	

Short answers: Do we have to wear a formal dress? – Yes, we do.
– No, we don't.

Must

→ **For things that we are obliged to do**

You must calm down. Or the bad guys will find us.

Police officers must arrest thieves. It's their duty.

→ **For recommendations**

Skyfall is one of the best James Bond films. You must watch it!

You must buy this dress. It's perfect for you.

Can't

→ **For things that we are prohibited from doing**

You can't smoke here. It's against the school rules.

I can bike here, but I can't drive here.

Police officers can arrest criminals, but they can't do it without proof.

Can we park here? — No, you can't. There's a parking lot over there.

Exercise 1 **Fill in the blanks with the correct form of *have to, must, can*.**

1. A: Do I (   ) (   ) finish this report today?

   B: Yes, you (   ). It's due tomorrow.

2. A: (   ) I (   ) (   ) bring the document to the office?

   B: No, (   ) (   ). You can send it by e-mail.

3. A: You (   ) come to the party with me. I need you!

   B: No, I (   ) (   ) study for the test tonight.

4. A: We (   ) take pictures of this painting, right?

   B: Sorry, sir. You (   ). Please put your camera in your bag.

Exercise 2 **Change the sentences to the negative sentences.**

e.g., *We can swim in this river.* → *We can't swim in this river.*

1. You can smoke in many restaurants these days.

   (   )

2. We can park the car here.

   (   )

3. I can play instruments in this apartment.

   (   )

Exercise 3 **Change the sentences by following the directions.**

e.g., *He has to go to school earlier.*

Question: Does he have to go to school earlier?

Negative: He doesn't (does not) have to go to school earlier.

1. I have to take off my shoes here.

   Question: (   )

2. He has to apologize to her.

   Question: (   )

3. They have to take the exam.

   Negative: (   )

4. Olive doesn't have to obey the order.

   Positive: (   )

Exercise 4 **Use the prompts and make sentences with *must*.**

e.g., *You / read all the books → You must read all the books.*

1. I / study harder

   (   )

2. you / try the bakery near this campus

   (   )

3. the police officer / examine the reason carefully

   (   )

4. students in this class / be nice to each other

   (   )

Exercise 5 **These are some school rules. Fill in the blanks with *can/can't/ must/ don't have to*.**

1. Students (   ) come to class on time.
2. Students (   ) play with their phones during class.
3. Students (   ) listen quietly when the teacher is speaking.
4. Students (   ) turn on the air conditioner in the summer.
5. Students (   ) join a club activity if they don't want to.

Speaking Activity

Exercise 1.1

Ask and answer the following questions with your partner(s):

1. Do you want to go abroad?
2. Where do you want to go?
3. When do you want to go?
4. Who do you want to go with?

Exercise 1.2

Discuss airport rules with your partner(s). Write the rules in the space below.

Rules:

You have to have a flight ticket.

Useful expressions: batteries, spray cans, knives, passport, check-in

Exercise 1.3

Read the following comments. What advice would you give in these situations?

1. I got to the airport, but I can't find my passport.
2. There is a long line at security. I will miss my flight.
3. My connecting flight is delayed. I have 10 hours before my next flight.
4. My flight is at 3 AM. There is no train to take me to the airport.
5. I get very nervous on the airplane.

Role Play

CD: Track 44

Blair: Hi, Akiko! Can I talk to you for a moment?

Akiko: Sure. What's up?

Blair: I'm visiting Tokyo this summer. I don't know what to do or where to go.

Akiko: Okay. What kinda thing do you wanna do?

Blair: Well, I'm a real foodie and love shopping.

Akiko: Maybe you can go to Omotesando. There are plenty of high-end stores there.

Blair: Hmm, that sounds expensive. I'm on a budget.

Akiko: Then you must go to Harajuku. There's a lot of cute shops and instagrammable food stalls.

Blair: Awesome! I'll do that! Thanks, Akiko.

Akiko: Have a nice trip.

USEFUL EXPRESSIONS
IN CONVERSATION

What's up?
kinda
wanna
foodie
high-end stores
on a budget
instagrammable
food stall
Awesome!
Have a nice trip.

Review 2

1 Let's practice comparative and superlative adjectives.

Look at the following table, and compare the countries with your partner(s).

e.g. *Russia is larger than China. China is the smallest of the three countries.*

Size

Country	Size
Russia	17,100,000 km^2
United States	980 km^2
China	960 km^2

Population

Country	Population
China	1,400,000,000
India	1,350,000,000
United States	324,000,000

Average temperature

Country (City)	Max	Min
Russia (Vladivostok)	19.8°C	−12.3°C
Canada (Montreal)	21.0°C	−10.1°C
China (Beijing)	26.7°C	−3.1°C

2 Let's practice present simple, past simple, present continuous, present perfect, and *will*.

Malala

Malala Yousafzai [1](be) a Pakistani activist for female education. Since age 11, she [2](express) her feelings for girls' right to education. On 9th October, 2012, a Taliban gunman [3](shoot) her. Luckily, she [4](recover). In 2014, she [5](win) the Nobel Prize for her courage and hard work. At the moment, she [6](continue) her work through Malala Fund. This fund [7](give) education to many girls in countries such as India and Latin America. She [8](be) one of the most inspirational women today, and as she is young, she [9](do) many more great things in the future.

1. (   )   2. (   )   3. (   )

4. (   )   5. (   )   6. (   )

7. (   )   8. (   )   9. (   )

3 Let's practice *have to*.

The following memo is Martin's to-do list for this week. Make sentences with *have to* for ☐ items. Make sentences with *don't have to* for ☑ items.

e.g. *He has to make documents for the next meeting.*
He doesn't have to e-mail Mr Tanaka about the next conference.

To-do list

☐ make documents for the next meeting
☑ e-mail Mr Tanaka about the next conference
☑ file the secret documents in a cabinet
☐ hold a meeting with the clients
☐ buy a carton of milk
☑ call Olivia about the next date

4 Let's practice *can't*.

Look at the signs below. Where do you see these signs? Take turns saying what you can't do.

e.g., *You can't drink alcohol at the school cafeteria.*
Don't drink alcohol at the school cafeteria.

5 Let's practice *can*.

What kind of robot do you want? Tell your partner(s) all the things that your robot can do.

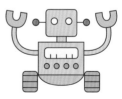

e.g. *The name of my robot is Housekeeper. First, it can clean my room. Second, it can make dinner every day. We can live a comfortable life with its help.*

6 Let's practice imperative.

Look at the recipes for pancakes below. Take turns explaining each step.

e.g., *Add six cups of pancake mix, two eggs and a cup of milk into a bowl.*

Useful expressions:

> add, mix, pour, flip, serve, egg, pancake mix, bowl, frying pan, plate

7 Let's practice *must* (recommendation).

 CD: Track 45

This is a conversation between two people. Practice the conversation with your partner. Then practice the conversation again by changing the underlined words.

A: I will travel to Paris this summer.

B: Really? I went there last year.

A: Where do you recommend?

B: You must go to Eiffel tower.

A: Why?

B: The night view from the tower is awesome.

A: Where else?

B: How about the Louvre museum? You can see a lot of famous paintings and sculptures.

A: Wow, they sound interesting.

B: You must visit these places.

オリーブ・グリーン：
ミステリードラマで学ぶ実用英語（CEFR-A1）

検印
省略   ©2021 年 1 月 31 日　　第 1 版発行

編著者　　　　　　　　　　　浅利　庸子
　　　　　　　　　　　　　　菅野　　悟
　　　　　　　　　　　　　　久保　岳夫
　　　　　　　　　　　　　　佐藤　亮輔

発行者　　　　　　　　　　　原　　雅　久
発行所　　　　　　　　株式会社 朝日出版社
　　　　　　　〒101-0065 東京都千代田区西神田 3-3-5
　　　　　　　　電話　東京　(03) 3239-0271
　　　　　　　　FAX　東京　(03) 3239-0479
　　　　　　　E-mail　text-e@asahipress.com
　　　　　　　　振替口座　00140-2-46008
　　　　　　　　http://www.asahipress.com/
　　　　　　組版／メディアアート　製版／図書印刷

乱丁・落丁本はお取り替えいたします。
ISBN 978-4-255-15674-3